Wiser & Wilder

A Soulful Path for Visionary Women Entrepreneurs

Kaya Singer

Awakening Business Press

1728 NE Highland Street Portland, Oregon 97211

kaya@kayasinger.com

The artwork and illustrations by Kaya Singer
Cover painting by Kaya Singer

Book design by Deandra Ellerbe, DeMicaro Designs, Portland, Oregon

Library of Congress Control Number: 2015959329

ISBN 978-0-9826412-2-4

I dedicate this book to the millions of Wise and Wild women who are, right in this moment, transforming the world to be a more peaceful, loving place.

MORE PRAISE FOR WISER AND WILDER

"If I had only had this book when I left corporate America in pursuit of creating a fulfilling business, my path would have been so much easier and faster towards the success I enjoy today. *Wiser and Wilder* guides you from inspiration through effective business know-how to nurture your highest vision into reality—in a way the feeds your woman's soul! "

Sonia Miller, Author of *The Attraction Distraction: Why the Law of Attraction Isn't Working for You and How to Get Results*

"It was beyond refreshing to read and experience the charm, simplicity, and powerful wisdom offered in Kaya Singer's soulful book *Wiser and Wilder*. The twenty-first century has arrived just in time to help us reframe the way we do business, protect earth resource, and honor age. Kaya's visionary expertise is more than timely, highlighting a joyful approach toward personal abundance and illustrated with her whimsical art. The book urges the reader to shift their consciousness toward a new paradigm; one that combines joy, business, and health as a triad for success."

Isha Lerner, Author of *Inner Child Cards: A Fairy Tale Tarot* and *The Triple Goddess Tarot*

"Kaya's journey along with information not far from being Shamanic enriched is very empowering. *Wiser and Wilder* takes us back to our roots as women, back to who we truly are before we felt dis-empowered. A great book to grow from."

Mia Saenz, Editor-in-Chief, *BellaMia Magazine*

"*Wiser and Wilder* is a book that will tap you on the shoulder, inviting you to go deep into your heart and soul. Being a woman in business is a very different experience from what many of us expect. Kaya Singer shares a vision of doing business, and life, in a round, whole, integrated, and uniquely feminine way. The information on the three stages of life and business should be required reading for every woman who wants to make a difference and a living."

Lynne Klippel, Best-selling Author of *Overcomers, Inc.*

"Kaya Singer's soul opens on every page of *Wise and Wilder*. Though I've been on my spiritual and emotional growth journey many years, I recognized places within me where I'm still, growing and need to release past hurts that's impacted my creativity and my business. I see myself as fairly confident and her empowerment rituals are helping me embrace my greatness and believe in my brilliance on an even higher level. A must-read for creative women entrepreneurs."

Denise Michaels, Founder, International Book Writing Guild

Contents

Foreword

A Wild Woman is unafraid when her path becomes rough and overgrown. She embraces her wild feminine power. She acknowledges her wisdom which adorns her heart and mind. And she blossoms into a leader showing all women the path to walk.

— Shikoba

"A few years ago, I was looking for a new mentor and business coach, a woman with some wisdom and gray hair. Someone smart, but who would understand me, and get that I want, and need, to build my business differently.

Unfortunately, I couldn't find anyone that fit that description. So I hired Andrea."

This was how Kaya introduced me at a workshop she hosted in Portland, and it remains one of the most touching (and humbling!) introductions I've received, and I've had many in my 15+ years as an entrepreneur and speaker.

The thing is, I understand entirely what her dilemma was, and it is my honor to have coached her the last several years, despite the fact that I didn't meet her criteria. There are thousands of coaches in the world, but only very few who insist upon helping their clients build businesses from the inside, out. (Hint: When you don't do that, you end up with a business that doesn't fit you. You'll learn more about how costly this is in the pages that follow.)

There are even fewer coaches who understand feminine energy, the way Kaya does, having lived in an intentional community in NZ and helped run women's gatherings. Rarer still - and like diamonds they are, really - are the coaches who can teach you about the cycles of a woman's life, and how to turn those cycles into benefits in your work. How to fully embrace what it means to be a visionary woman entrepreneur and be very successful.

Young women, you can access your inner wise woman much sooner than you think, by making friends with your inner Crone. Older women, you can keep your maiden energy alive longer too, through practical exercises, and patient cultivation. Women of all ages: there is a great need - a thirst, and a yearning - for you to be brave, and seize your wilder and wiser self in your business. Kaya is a coach and mentor who knows all these things, and has, with a great belly full of love and wisdom, shared stories and exercises to help you on this path.

Just like her introduction, Kaya's book cuts through the B.S. She is, in fact, the mentor and coach of her own dreams, and perhaps yours as well - wise, wild, gray of hair, and full of vision and heart.

–Andrea J. Lee

Author, *We Need to Talk: Your Guide to Challenging Business Conversations*

Introduction

To begin, I'd like to share a bit about the winding path that has brought me to writing this book today.

It all began when I was 25 and hopped into my newly hand-painted yellow VW bus to head out West. I landed in Eugene, Oregon, where I started my very first business. The problem was I didn't know it was a business because I was on an adventure to figure out who I really was.

I grew up in the 1950s in a middle class Midwestern city in Ohio. My dad went to work with his briefcase and my mom stayed home. Actually, all the moms stayed home in my neighborhood. Think of the TV commercials from that era with women wearing aprons in the kitchen. That was my house.

No one asked me what I wanted to do when I grew up because it was assumed I would get married to a 'good man' and he would have the career. I knew I could become a nurse or a teacher, but I saw most of those women quitting their jobs after they got married. I didn't know one woman who was an entrepreneur. I wasn't even exactly sure what that word meant, but I knew that if it existed, it was a male identity.

The boys in my high school class were already preparing for greatness.

Patrick O'Rouke was one of those. He ended up being the student body president in our senior year and eventually became the editor of the National Lampoon. You may have heard of him; he goes by P.J. O'Rourke now. It could be that he was simply smarter than I was, but I doubt it. More likely, because of our culture, he saw a path I didn't know was there.

Off I went to college in 1965, mainly because I grew up in a Jewish family that believed in educating their children. It didn't matter if college was going to lead to a career or not, which it wasn't from their point of view. No, it wasn't about what I was going to major in or if I was going to find a good job. In fact, I was told to major in education so that I could be a teacher in case my husband died.

Yes, I am serious.

I didn't have a clue what I wanted to do in college, so I did art because it was one thing I liked. The second term was when I discovered ceramics. I hadn't known what having a passion was until then. It was like a big light switch turned on and I spent hours in the ceramics lab making things out of clay. Every night, I went down to the lab to work, taking clay from Mother Earth and turning it into something useful and beautiful. Putting it into the fire and seeing what came out was like magic. It was still way before the 'woo-woo' era that came later in the 70s, but that was the beginning of a wake up call for me. Looking back on it now, I think that through the experience of molding the clay, I was molding myself, finding out who I was.

My college experience was also about gaining awareness of social change. As I was coming into myself through my clay work, I began seeing the world outside myself with new eyes too. It was the era of

Vietnam War protests, campus revolution and beginning to see the world in a new context. The political fervor around me grabbed my attention and I started having visions of the world I wanted to help create.

Yet, in the middle of all the craziness, campus riots and protests, there were also these geeky guys walking across campus with their briefcases on their way to their computer science classes. Guess who one of those people was? Bill Gates. He went to Ohio State at the same time as me, but I never looked at him or any of the other nerdy guys because briefcases weren't cool and I didn't even know what computer science was.

When I finally graduated with a degree in Fine Arts, I still had no idea of who I was except that I was someone who never wanted to work for someone else. I was a free spirit through and through. I wanted to enjoy life and not be confined to sitting in a cubicle somewhere and doing a job that was only about making money. I had such a narrow view of what work was and had no idea what business was, except that it was something that men did.

So I ended up staying in Eugene where I discovered Saturday Market. In a few weeks, I found a studio to make pottery and a spot in the market to sell it from orange crates. I was a potter selling her wares and having fun; I didn't identify with being an entrepreneur. I realized that I would much rather make and sell my pottery than work for someone else, yet I still didn't realize I was running a business.

I made and sold ceramics for seven years and financially I did okay with it, but because I didn't really understand it was a business, I never really learned how to run it like a business. I did discover that if I wanted to sell ten pieces, I needed more than ten, more like a hundred because people need a choice. But there were so many things I didn't get because of my limited point of view, especially the fact that I never looked for business help.

So when my back started hurting and I couldn't throw pots for eight hours a day anymore, I decided to quit. I knew there were people who sold pottery and made a lot more money than I did, but I just thought they were better potters than I was. I could have hired someone to do the parts I couldn't do, but I didn't have a business mindset, so I didn't know that people who own businesses don't do all the work themselves. It didn't occur to me to stay with it and make changes so it could continue on and possibly grow into something larger.

That was my huge blind spot.

Fifteen years later, after divorces and new marriages and a Master's degree in counseling, I moved to New Zealand with my new husband and my then teenage son. That's where I finally experienced an inner transformation about the world of money.

Money had never been important in my life. I always had had 'enough' to just get by, but I was almost 50 by then and wanted to make some real money. Since I had been avoiding the whole world of money, thinking I wasn't smart enough for so long, I wasn't sure of where to begin, but I somehow knew that it was time to grow up and do my business for real. So I began searching for mentoring, but all I could find was business help geared to men.

That left me feeling like I had to figure it all out by myself.

At the same time, I was a woman on the verge of menopause in a world that glorifies youth in women. Like anyone in transition, I had my share of letting go on a number of levels, including saying goodbye to my younger self, but I still wasn't ready to be perceived as 'old.' What to do?

I wasn't sure but I didn't give up. Instead, I danced in the sand with my women's circles and started a part-time counseling practice, which turned into coaching. I wasn't concentrating on work as such, but I discovered I was good at going to a strange place with strange people and attracting lots of clients. I didn't realize it, but that was my start.

Marketing is about connecting with people and that's what I did, but I knew I needed more than marketing. I wanted to get to the next step and really understand the world of business, so I started looking for business help that spoke not just to women, but to women in my life stage, ideally a woman entrepreneur who was older than me who could give me support and tell me I wasn't crazy or stupid.

I met that person at a weeklong women's gathering. Across the circle from me sat Barbara, a woman my age who owned a highly successful art gallery. I asked her to tell me how to make real money. She took a stick and drew a picture on the ground and said, "It's easy, just like growing a garden. You plant seeds, water them, nurture them and eventually they grow and flower. Planting money seeds works the same way."

This was 1994 and not one book I had read explained business this way. This was a woman's way of looking at the world explained in language that I could understand.

Later, I hired a woman business coach, but she didn't get it either. I told her I helped solo entrepreneurs with marketing and she said if I wanted to grow a real business, I would starve because those people wouldn't be able to pay me. (I hope you are laughing as you read this.) She advised me to quit and go into executive coaching. I had never spent even one day in the corporate world. I had been a potter and then a counselor. What did I know about corporate executives?

This coach may have been a woman, but she was also just one more person who was trying to force me into a box that didn't fit. Luckily, Barbara's words stuck with me. What she told me felt right while everything else felt wrong, like a man's suit I was trying on that just didn't fit, so I persisted and experimented. Through trial and error, I finally figured out how to plant those seeds in my own garden and learned what it would take to make them grow.

If you are any kind of gardener, you will know that gardening is a lot of work, but the main ingredients are love, attitude, persistence, sunlight, water and your clear vision. Two decades later, and now on the Wise Woman side of menopause, I get that my experiences are my gift to present and future women. My purpose and passion is to share what I've learned with women of all ages who are also motivated by a vision that lives deep in their souls. There is a yearning to follow your calling, make a difference, create your own footprint and also make money.

The world is different now. There are more women in the working world than ever before and there are lots of women entrepreneurs, so young women are seeing their mothers running businesses. But women are still women, and a woman's way of doing business is still very new. The idea that you can follow your Wild Woman's passion, stay in balance, raise your children and create a business that will make enough money to support you in your Wise Woman years when you just might be doing your real work well, that's still new.

I wish someone had told me this and given me the steps to make it happen. That's why I'm about to share them with you. **This book will walk you down your own soulful path and will require you to call forth your Wild Woman from wherever she has been hiding in wait.**

The path will ask you to trust the innate wisdom that lives in your heart. You will be called to listen to your intuition and insight that runs powerfully with your blood until it runs no more and you become Wise Woman and Crone Woman, the one who has presence and inner sight.

Yes, this is not your usual business book. Instead, it is a book about how to be, how to thrive and how to flourish on your own visionary path.

A Woman's Way

"I began my business while I still had my job, so I was still doing things the more masculine way, which had made me successful in the corporate world where a strong drive, big goals and high ambition get you somewhere.

Even though I was very successfully climbing the corporate ladder, something was not right, so I began to search and followed my instincts towards becoming a coach. When I did my first coach training, I felt like I had found my home and remember thinking, "These are my people." At the age of 29, I realized I could have a new vision for my life that included following my own values and being authentic, instead of just doing what I thought was the right thing to do.

I still have ambition, like I did in my first career, but I have learned how to use it as a more feminine leader. I now prefer a softer, more creative and intuitive approach. This is the energy I think the world needs more of, but I had undervalued those parts of myself for a long time, so I had to relearn how to use them. Stepping into those places has been a huge part of what has helped my business to grow.

When I developed The Right Brain Business Plan, it came from that place inside of myself that called for following a vision and being creative in an intuitive feminine way."

~Jennifer Lee

Jennifer's story reflects what I have heard from hundreds of women who realized they were stifling their natural woman ways by trying to fit into a box where they didn't belong. They thought the only way to success was to get a high-powered job and do well at it, not realizing that there was another pathway to follow, their true feminine way.

In these first two chapters, we'll be looking at what it really means to have success the women's way and how this takes you right back to who you are as women, your innate strengths and your natural feminine attributes. As you read about the three facets of a Woman's Way, you will likely breathe a sigh of relief. What a comfort to know that your roots are already firmly planted in this woman's world and you only have to be a more fully actualized version of yourself, which is not only acceptable but also needed to create real change.

Reclaiming the Woman's Way

Certain ways of being are inherent in women. Rebecca Skeele, one of my colleagues, calls this the Divine Feminine. I call it your Wise and Wild Woman. Whatever we call it, it's those parts of a woman's psyche that need to be acknowledged and appreciated for the value of what they bring to the world.

Reclaiming the Woman's Way is about each of you retrieving your soul, your Wise and Wild Woman who is meant to be part of you as your partner. This process involves allowing her intrinsic presence to permeate your being as you take her core values into your work in the world through your service and your own entrepreneurial creation.

Once you cultivate and grow a more authentic version of yourself, you begin to realize it's not all about you; it's also about global change and knowing that these values are what the world needs right now. As a leader of your own business, you have the deep opportunity to step into this partnership where your inner self unites with your vision for the world. This unity will enable you to build your business based on your own values and to recognize that your Wise and Wild Woman is with you everyday. All you have to do is call on her, ask her for her wisdom, ideas and point of view, and then listen.

I remember the Dali Lama saying, "The world will be saved by Western women." The beginning of this shift can absolutely be seen with today's female visionary entrepreneurs who not only want to follow their passion but also make a bigger difference.

Three Facets of a Woman's Way

The Woman's Way is meant to coexist in harmony with the ways of her male counterpart. It is not about polarizing or discounting the values that are more male oriented. Certainly, there is tremendous value in scientific thinking, focused power and even competition at times. However, those traits on their own, without the feminine partner, are out of balance. The affects of this can be seen in our government and some large corporate businesses where there appears to be a lack of heart, an overgrowth of greed and a shortage of compassion.

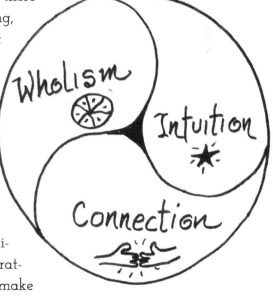

When we look more closely at the feminine qualities, it's easier to see how operating with these values at the helm can make such a difference.

WHOLISM

Wholism speaks to women's natural ability to see the connection between different parts of a system and how one decision will affect many others. This heightened awareness enables women to see the whole picture and make decisions from this mindfulness. You've heard people say how women are naturally good at multi-tasking. Multi-tasking can be stressful, but women do have this ability to juggle many pieces at once. They naturally see the whole picture. This is helpful in business as well as personal life.

A women's way is to consider how their business choices affect their family, health, values and lifestyle because they are all connected.

It's not natural for most women to put on blinders and just focus on work like an arrow going toward a target, while ignoring how they feel, their relationships, their energy or their purpose.

I sometimes wonder if plastic containers, which have created so much pollution and toxicity around the world, would ever have been developed if women had been part of the development team. They may have brought in a more wholistic consciousness to look at the entire picture, including what would happen to these containers after they were used or how they affect human bodies. There are thousands of similar examples that illustrate what happens when this wholistic viewpoint is not being valued.

This is why I love mandalas so much, because their circles with a multitude of pieces all fit together to make a healthy whole.

How you do one thing needs to overlap into how you do everything. This is part of a beingness which is part of our innate psyches.

My office walls are filled with pie charts and mind mapping because I have learned that on a wholistic level I need to see the bigger picture. If I start a project and ignore some of the pie pieces, I begin to feel stressed and uneasy because the information that lives in those unseen areas actually might affect the part I am working on now.

Every time I ignore this truth and try to focus on just one piece of the pie too long, I become Crazy Woman, get depressed and feel like quitting. I often use the words 'off center' to describe that feeling.

It reminds me of throwing pots. It's mystical, taking that lump of clay, putting it in on a spinning wheel, and from a place of feeling centered inside myself, my hands connect with the heart and soul of the clay and like magic, it centers itself on the wheel. Only then can I turn it into any beautiful shape I choose. If it's not centered, I can't do anything with it and it could even fly off the wheel and go splat on the floor. It feels as if the spirit of the clay knows that its every molecule needs to be touched and included.

I've found that the trick for me is to tune inward everyday when I begin work and see myself as this piece of clay that needs to be whole and centered in every part of myself. From this place, I can create, coach, support, write, manage money or whatever, and it flows from a place of spirit. All those pieces stay connected and aligned.

Remembering that you are wholistically oriented will help you deal with anything that comes up in your life that impacts your visionary business. It will help you respond with an open heart and from a sense of peace.

Women need to be with their inner world, in body, mind, spirit and heart, before they can be their best in the outer world because these two mirror each other. You will work way more effectively when you are centered, tuned in and accessing all of the parts of yourself that make you a whole woman.

You may feel unwell if you attempt to ignore certain parts of yourself in order to get things done faster, or try to get them over with so you can get back to what you love. It's impossible to do good work from this place, because as women, we automatically see how everything is tied together.

I noticed myself falling into that out of balance space a couple times while writing this book. I just wanted to get it done and was totally in my head. From that place, what I wrote was crap. I hated it and deleted it all later. It lacked the energy I wanted to communicate. I was tired and my real voice wasn't what came out. It was the clay going splat over and over again.

This happened on one of my writing retreats where I had to keep going for walks on the beach to try and re-center myself. The ocean is one of my natural homes; for me, it is the direct opposite of being in a cage. After being on the beach and walking, walking, walking, my insides would get realigned and balanced and I could feel the shift happening.

What are the things that you do that to keep yourself aligned or help you get realigned? It is so important to know what those things are because they need to become part of your health and wellness practice.

A woman's way is also to put your children first and make decisions from that place, but the corporate model expects you to put your job first. I know a woman who was asked in an interview, "Can you put in long hours and work into the evening if necessary?" She thought about her small children at home and also thought about the paycheck and struggled. She knew she wouldn't get the job if she didn't answer yes and if she took the job and then had to stay home with a sick child, she would be judged as not being committed enough. What a horrible position to be put in. The question came from someone who was not valuing this woman for her gifts; instead, it was only about one piece of the pie.

Based on this traditional model, some people have the opinion that you won't be successful at business if you are a mother. Again, that is polarizing rather than wholistic thinking.

Women are more willing to grow their businesses slower, work fewer hours, travel less and keep their business intentionally smaller while their kids are little. I've worked with many such moms and we develop a business plan based on the ages of their kids, where they can eventually work more as their children grow older. Eventually there will be no kids at home and your business tree, with its strong root system, will provide lots of opportunity for growth.

Many women become entrepreneurs for this reason. It's an opportunity to create a new model. One of the best parts of owning your own business is that you set the values for your company. From a wholistic point of view, you value health, well-being and family because they will help support your business success for many years with ease.

INTUITION

The women's way of doing business begins with emotions and intuition. Ideas percolate on the inner planes and feelings emerge way before thoughts. Women's knowing lives in their womb, the energetic and physical place of birth.

Rebecca Skeele shares that because she has an open heart and is very sensitive, she used to be swamped with feelings. She used to react from that place, but then she learned how to glean information from her feelings, which eventually opened channels to her intuition or what she refers to as Divine Guidance. She says that this 'energy in motion' allows her to open to her higher intuitive mind. She now runs her business from this place as well as her whole life.

You will appreciate Rebecca's sharing if you are someone who can get off track and feel like you are drowning in your emotions. The important piece is learning to gain the insight from those emotions that come up. This has been a life-long practice for me and there are still times when I feel like a piece of clay that is off center and very wobbly.

Like Rebecca, I have developed my own process of diving right into the mud, as I call it. Whether it's fears, confusion or any other emotions that feel big, I choose to go straight into it and from that place I talk to my Wise Woman and ask what's going on. She is the one who is quietly always present in the roots of my tree. I ask her, "what do I need to know or understand?" Once I listen and hear, I begin to sense my inner sight opening and awareness comes streaming through. The clay of my being becomes centered again.

All business is about taking risks, but it is less risky when you have done this inner work first.

We, as women, are also so deeply connected to the moon and our monthly cycles during our fertile years. Although women have been the brunt of so many negative jibes around being moody or overly emotional when they are pre-menstrual, in fact, this is the time when intuition and insight are often the strongest. At this time of each month, you may feel an open doorway to your inner power. You may be more emotional, but some of those feelings can actually lead the way to deeper intuitive understanding. Now that I am on the Wise Woman side of menopause, that doorway is open most of the time.

Michelle Grace Lesserad, shamanic teacher, shared with me that she has a process that involves tapping into this greater intuition using the phases of the moon. She says, "The new moon is the perfect time to ask 'How am I blocked?' Then when the full moon comes, I always get my answer." The moon is the fastest moving body out there and as women we spend our fertile years and beyond connected to her energies. It is nature's way of providing support.

Women often drown in the negative side of their own emotions and get stuck there. I'm referring to self-doubt, lack of confidence, fears and all that other crud that keeps you confused and struggling. It's a mistake to make any decisions from this place because those reactive decisions will come from fear or worry instead of from your connection to your real feminine truth, your intuition and inner sight. It's so important to learn the skills to transform the negative emotions, get the deep message and then make the decision from this new awareness. If you don't learn to transform your emotions into insight, they can be debilitating.

Sharing your feelings and asking for help is safe in our women's culture whereas, in the corporate culture, having feelings of doubt and asking for help can be construed as "not knowing." Somehow that can get twisted into making you look bad because you need help. This is one reason women feel safer in women's circles where it feels easier to say "I don't understand" or "I don't know how" and not feel judged.

Many years ago I did some training with Elizabeth Kubler-Ross, the doctor who pioneered bringing death and dying out of the closet. The room was filled with a hundred people who were trying to recover from terrible losses and abuse. She taught processes that were about externalizing emotions by screaming, pounding things and ripping up phone books. At first, being in the room was scary to me because people seemed so out of control and I wondered if they were okay.

However, I discovered that after I did one of these sessions myself my mind was clearer, my intuition was stronger and I could see my situation in a whole new light. At one time I was someone who always wanted to look like I had it together and showing those kinds of emotions was hard for me. I worried that people would judge me as not being competent. It's the opposite now. When I see a woman willing to bare her soul and go right into the muck and do the work, I trust her a lot more because I know she is going to be very clear and open as a result.

- How do you lose yourself in your emotions?
- What do you do to help your emotions transmute to greater intuition or insight?
- How would operating in this way help you in your business?

CONNECTION

Relationships, community and collaboration live at the core of a woman's way of running a business.

Competition implies a polarity where there are winners and losers. In collaboration, everyone wins. The women's way of leading a team is by encouraging cooperation and honoring each person's contribution. The goal is to create a program or an event that is awesome and provides help for many people.

Nancy quit her corporate job after a male team member talked over her in a loud voice in a meeting and stole her idea. This wasn't the first time it happened so she spoke up, but the manager ignored her and did nothing. On her team points were given for having good ideas, so she lost out again. She said there were no points given for collaboration, working together or sharing ideas, which were all the things she was good at.

When she later shared her frustration with the manager privately, he defended the other man and said he had balls and she needed to learn to be more aggressive if she wanted to succeed. The next day she handed in her resignation. Then she began her own business that she runs based on the values she is aligned with.

We are now in the age of relationship and interaction marketing, so its women's time to shine! Women are naturally relationship oriented and tend to want to give and offer support. The feminine way is to empathize and care.

Social media is all about connecting and having meaningful conversations. These relationship skills are so needed now. This includes compassionate listening, offering help and building connections, all things that are so important in running a business.

In Chapter 3 I will share more fully about how to develop a circle around yourself that includes all these things that offer you support and empowerment.

What Makes a Women's Way so Valuable?

Women need other women. Women have been supporting each other for eons, whether around quilting bees or sitting around the fire making tortillas. It's in our genes to sit in circle with other women.

Understanding the Woman's Way of business can help you to tap into the core of who you are and to know you don't have to change yourself to fit anyone else's picture of how you should be. You are more likely to be successful when you are operating in harmony with your inner self and really listening to your inner wisdom.

Begin by integrating wholism, intuition and connection into your vision as integral parts of your core values. Doing this will help you to re-claim your soul, replenish your hunger and reinstate your inherent connection with your Wise and Wild Woman.

Accept who you are, your gifts and your ways of being in the world. It is so needed right now. It's my belief that if all women really stepped into their power and began to operate from this place as a universal group, the affects would be resounding.

Take a look at the chart below to compare what happens if you operate from a stuck and separated place to how different it is when you do it the Wise Woman's way.

What happens when women get stuck and remain separated from their Wise and Wild Woman:	Benefits of uniting with the Woman's Way approach:
Trying to be more conventional in order to fit in	Celebrating your colorful and innovative self
Comparing themselves to other people who appear to be more successful	Opening your voice and sharing your unique story
Feeling overwhelmed with all the work involved in running their own business	Beginning with balance and listening to your intuition
Focusing only on what they like doing and avoiding things they don't like or understand	Shifting into holistic mindset which effects how you do everything
Not seeing the path to growing larger, so staying small and stuck	Nurturing a business like a relationship
Getting lost in fear and self-doubt and making decisions from that place	Learning your own process for transmuting emotions into heightened intuition

Over the last 20 years, I have been connecting with a large community of spirited entrepreneurial women who are creating a very different model, a true Woman's Way of doing business. Because of the freedom to control the values and culture they are creating, they have been able to venture forth and design a new path to success supported by a feminine vision of doing business. Some have even stepped out and started innovative businesses without having a clue about what they were doing. They just knew they had a vision and a strong calling to help people by putting their voice into the world in a bigger way. You'll be hearing from many of them in the following chapters as they share their stories.

Are you ready to be part of a movement with other women who are saying yes to the Woman's Way of business?

Not only will this help you to create the success you want, but you will be modeling this approach for the next generation of women.

Your Woman's Way Mandala

Use the template on the following page to create your own mandala. The three intersecting circles represent the three facets of the Woman's Way and your strengths in each area.

Use colored pencils or markers of your choice to fill in each area. Make it your own by responding to the questions below that will help you access words to write in each section.

Then, on the outside of the mandala, make note of the ways you want to grow or expand in each of the areas.

Wholism
- How do you use your natural ability to see the whole picture?
- How does this support your life and/or business in a positive way?
- How could you develop and bring this in even more?

Intuition
- How do your emotions and intuition help you in your life and/or business?
- How do you transmute your emotions and then get greater insight?
- When you get stuck in debilitating emotions, how do you shift this?

Connection
- How do your strong relationship skills support your success?
- What are your natural and easy ways for developing positive community?
- How do you collaborate for greater benefit?

When you are done, give thanks to your Wise Woman for helping you acknowledge your natural Woman's Way of being.

Go to WiserandWilder.com/resources to download a full page template and also see samples of what others have done.

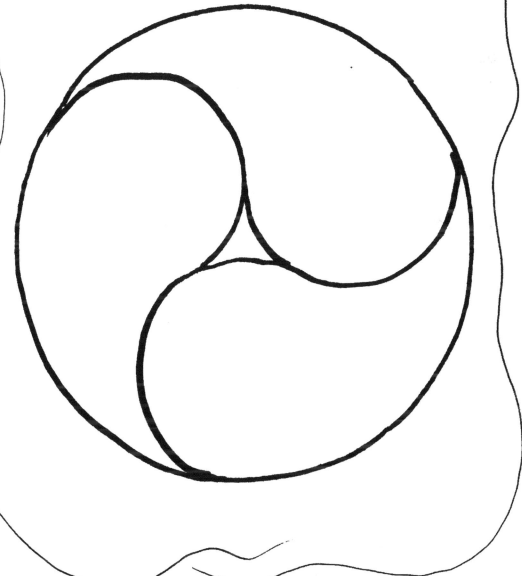

CHAPTER TWO

Back to Your Roots

"I was the oldest child of nine and my mom was a stay-at-home mother while my dad was the 'hard worker.' Like many fathers of that era, he discouraged me from doing my own thing, telling me instead to get a stable job, such as becoming a secretary. Those were the avenues open to women in those days, before feminism became more mainstream.

So I entered a male dominated workforce and gave it my all, but eventually I became exhausted by the intense competition and high-powered sales model at my workplace. I was good at my work and had accounts with big name companies like Gucci and Calvin Klein, but my work wasn't good for me or the divine feminine part of my soul. I hadn't yet realized that I could stand in my own vision and do the real work I was meant to do in the world, my way. My birth order (first child) probably helped me develop as a leader, and I also knew I was destined to be independent. Maybe that's why I had the courage to find a more nurturing career path for myself.

Now I am not at all about competition. Instead, I am all about relationships and women supporting each other, being authentic and being what I call your Intrepid Self."

~Katie Cavanough

Katie's story reminds us that no matter how far off track you have gone, you can always find your way back to your true self, your roots and your inherent feminine being. In this chapter we'll look at some of the most important steps you can take to begin your courageous journey back to yourself, including opening your voice, welcoming your Wild Woman and being authentic. Let's begin with refocusing.

Focus on Feminine Values

This book is all about re-focusing on how to be more true to yourself. It is built on the belief that there is no right or wrong way to be; there is only your way which supports and allows you to live your life fully. Shifting your focus to the feminine values of the Woman's Way is the first step because from there you can stand in a place of your own truth.

The culture we live in teaches women like Katie, plus many other visionary women, to believe that success is all about getting a job in a high-powered company. For some women, it's not until they become fully immersed in that world that they realize they are women in a masculine culture and that their own genuine vision needs a different environment in order to emerge.

It's important to not polarize and see the masculine model as being wrong or bad and the feminine way as being good and right. For a long time, the masculine model was the only option out there and the three facets I shared in the first chapter were under-valued, so women found themselves in an environment that said you must not only be better than someone else, you must also outdo yourself. This driven, focused approach doesn't work for many women who can't survive and thrive in that kind of environment. Over the years, I have seen it is a rare woman who can live well in that culture because it takes such a heavy toll on their health, wellness and feminine natures.

One woman who worked for a large company surrounded by male engineers would go to her office after management meetings and call me, her coach, and sob on the phone. Gradually, I helped her to bring more of her true self into her workplace by exploring and integrating the three facets of a Woman's Way (Chapter 1). But in the end, she resigned from her high paying, prestigious job anyway, and began her own business. I liken this experience to trying to grow a lovely rose in sandy soil; it just isn't the right environment. I've spoken to hundreds of women who, like this one, felt they had to leave their jobs or die. That's the beginning of a wake-up call.

So sit back, feel into your focused feminine nature, and then consider how taking the next three steps could help you become the empowered leader you are meant to be.

STEP 1: OPENING YOUR VOICE

What does it mean to have a voice? It means energizing and opening your throat chakra, the place of personal expression, power and choice. It means you have opinions, points of view and rants. Having a voice can mean: standing up and speaking out, telling your story and being funny, trusting, being authentic or daring to be exposed. Speaking up requires knowing that your unique voice is different from anyone else's and what you have to say counts and is needed.

So many women hold back, thinking they need to get it totally perfect first, but of course, there is no perfect. There is only your real life story, your truth and your wisdom, all of which are inherently worthwhile. The problem with waiting for it to be perfect is that you may never feel it's perfect enough, and during that waiting time, you are invisible, small and repressed. Your throat chakra is closed and the world never hears your message.

Some of my women clients have hired me to help them with marketing because, although they have no challenge with delivering high value service to their clients, they are extremely challenged with marketing which requires being seen, putting your voice out into the world and letting go of the privacy where you feel more comfortable. When I hear their fears, I can't help but wonder if they are tuning into the collective unconscious of our female ancestors, women who were killed for being outspoken, communicating their ideas and having strong viewpoints. Those fears also make them question if they have anything worthwhile to say.

Recently, I saw Monica Lewinsky's Ted Talk. She spoke about how at age 22, she fell in love with President Clinton while she was an intern at the White House. We all know what happened next; suddenly, the whole world had access to her most private life, including oral sex!

Obviously, Monica made some mistakes that caused her character to be smeared across the entire world where she was portrayed as a slut and a bimbo, plus a string of other horrible assaults on her character. Meanwhile, President Clinton went on to win a second term in office while Monica disappeared, along with her voice. We never heard from her until at age 40, almost 20 years later, when she reappeared not only with a powerfully strong voice for all women who have been unable to express themselves after a trauma, but to show the world how a woman can transform and be reborn from the ashes.

I cried when I watched that video. I was so happy she was finally speaking her truth. It reminded me of when I was 20 and propositioned by my married film teacher in a car on the way back from a conference. I thought he had invited me to go because he liked my work, but in fact he had other ideas. I was shocked and felt there was no one to tell. When I did get up the courage to talk to our department head, he ultimately did nothing.

Women like Monica and me, along with millions of others, learned that it's easier to keep our mouths shut and just hold our feelings inside. Some of us have since had the opportunity to learn how to scream in a safe place and be ok with the sound that emerged from our throats. Screaming can be horrifying; it can feel like there is a monster inside you that needs to come out of a cage. That's exactly what it felt like for me. **Ask any woman who feels trapped in a life that isn't feeding her soul.** Somewhere, her soul is still alive but it's not connected to her body. One woman told me she felt like a walking soulless women, disconnected from who she really was.

My personal story is like that of many women who grew up in the 50s and 60s. One of my vivid memories is of my mother always lying on the couch with a headache and me realizing at that moment that I had no idea why she was in pain or who she really was. I can see now that she felt weighted down and trapped in her life, a life she supposedly had chosen but didn't really choose. She could never talk about it because she repressed her feelings, but I knew she was unhappy without a word being said. Having no model, I grew up with no real voice myself. Instead, I would look at other people and try to copy what they did or said so I could fit in. It was horrible.

I do remember my free child when I was three or four; I think I knew who I was then, but no one asked and I had no words yet. By the time I was 10, I had no memory of those early years and had forgotten my true self, so I was afraid to speak out. I didn't really find out who I was until well into my adulthood. Although my voice is strong now, it took me until almost 60 years of age to really open that portal and find my Wild Woman, that part of me who feels okay in my own skin.

My friend, Nancy Swisher, a writer who is of my generation, has a similar story. Her father owned a grocery store and one day the milkman showed up and asked her that classic question, "What do you want to be when you grow up?" Her answer was, "I already am who I want to be."

She says she had such a clear awareness of who she was before it all got smothered by a life of trying to fit in and be what other people expected her to be.

Really, it all comes down to BEINGness - the authenticity of being who you really are. Only from that place can you open your voice and allow the world to see and hear you. But like Nancy, many of us have forgotten who we really are.

In order to take your vision into the world and allow it to grow, you have to be willing to stand on your soapbox and share your passionate mission and what lights you up. If you are a solopreneur and want to do it successfully, it has to be your voice coming through. You have to allow yourself to be seen and heard. Yet, over and over, I see women posting on social media or writing articles that sound like someone else. There is no life force because they are writing the way they think they need to, rather than just saying it the way it is for them.

- ◉ What do you have to say?
- ◉ What needs to come through your voice?
- ◉ What is the passion you want to express?

STEP 2: WELCOMING YOUR WILD WOMAN

Why have women always wanted and needed to be with each other? Often there's an unspoken understanding that when it's all women, you can let your hair down and talk about things that women intrinsically understand. Women have a bond with each other regardless of social class, political stance or religion. We all remember getting our first period, having sex for the first time, issues with our mothers or fathers, feeling lost and alone after a relationship break up, plus so many other things we share.

In my community in New Zealand, we had women's and men's gatherings. What the men did at their gathering was different than what we as women did, but the core result was the same in many ways. In both groups, everyone became more open, empowered and self-accepting. We got deeply in touch with our wildish natures. To do this as women, we focused on helping each other open our throat chakras, the place where we hold our true voice, so we could really BE who we need to be in this world.

When I left NZ and returned to the US, I decided to do my business for real. I felt really driven, but then it wasn't long before I felt my freedom and life force steadily diminishing because I was letting my business consume me. How did that happen? Now I realize I had left my Wild Woman in NZ wandering the beach in Wainui Bay (where I still wanted to be), while I was here in America trying to make money for the first time in my life.

Part of the Woman's Way of being in business is to have your Wild Woman, or wild feminine, as a business partner. She is your free spirit, busting with creativity, and the one who can take risks and follow her passion. She knows who you really are, your vision and your gifts. She dances, paints, speaks out, wears bright colors and goes for it! She helps you to connect with the other part of yourself, your Wise Woman. When you are able to quiet the noise and listen to this part of yourself you will know what your soul path is because it is she who holds the wisdom of your soul truth.

Eastern religions call this your dharma, what you came into the world with, including the natural abilities and inherent gifts you are destined to use in this lifetime. You may not know how to turn it into a business or how to express it, but you will know it's true. It can begin with acknowledging that what you are doing now has something missing. You have to trust the feelings and follow the thread.

It took me many years of painfully trying to run my business without my Wild Woman to realize I had cut off my joy and my community, so I felt like I was trapped, living in a cage. I only share this because we all can be missing something important even while doing our businesses. In some ways, the realizations that eventually come can be even more painful because we can't blame our jobs. We can only look inward to ourselves and realize that we abandoned our wild feminine partner somewhere along the way. In that process, your Wise Woman with her wisdom also become inaccessible.

Without your Wild Woman, you can become Stressed Out Woman or Fear Woman and live in a state of unhealthiness. I know I can share this with any woman and she will understand. Your story might be different but it will also be the same in so many ways. As women, we have our stories and this is what we do when we are together. **We talk and listen and talk some more and listen some more, thereby creating a web of support, love and inner knowing.**

Because this is such an important part of the Woman's Way, the stories I have heard from so many women are all about this piece. This is where the conversation begins. They explain their disconnect in their own language, but it's the same feeling of being out of alignment and missing a part of their soulful expression. Of course they come to me saying they want to get help growing their business, but I have to help them bring their Wild Woman on board first.

When I first started my business, I tried really hard to fit into a box that wasn't me. In my case, that box or cage told me to hide or ignore my emotions and instead wear 'businessy' clothes and cut my hair shorter. I also needed to hide my spiritual side, keep my family issues separate from my business and certainly not share my fears. These values, which I thought I was supposed to have, came from the male corporate business model.

No wonder I never wanted to acknowledge I had a business in my earlier years. I thought I would have to mold myself to fit into that box. Even though I never worked in a corporate environment, that image and message is now plastered all over the Internet and before that, it was everywhere in business journals and on TV too. This is what I thought business was; I thought I needed to look and be a certain way that was nothing like who I really was, and it certainly didn't include a Wild Woman, the part of each woman who just doesn't give a rip. She wears what she wants, dyes her hair blue, speaks her rant and couldn't care less if anyone likes or approves of her. She likes herself and that's what's most important.

My hair began to go grey when I was only 35. I began to dye it and did so for 10 years. I thought if I looked old, doors would be closed and people wouldn't take me seriously. The Old Woman archetype is very strong in our culture as someone who is haggard, dried up and not to be taken seriously. This is changing now with more women my age coming out of hiding, but it is still such a big influence. Young women have their hormones and sexy energy so there is a space for them, but old women have been placed at the bottom of the heap in our culture. I stopped dying my hair at age 50 because of the chemicals, but more importantly because I felt I needed to step up and face my life stage. It was hard at first because suddenly, almost overnight, people started seeing me as the age I really was instead of 10 years younger.

It was painful, because in our youth-focused culture, who was I to be? Plus, it was already challenging to have lost my young woman hormonal energy, which embodies sensual beauty in its archetypal form.

I continued to fight it until I finally realized that my silver hair could be a reflection of how I have stepped into the Wise Woman stage of life. Wise Woman is the one who holds your wisdom and has that deep inner sight. She quietly lives in your heart center. I really do see myself as an elder entrepreneur now and have fully embraced it and no longer want to hide it. It wasn't an easy transformation for me. It took me 10-15 years to fully accept it and understand that by not accepting it, I was cutting off my power source. This acceptance is also what gradually helped me to reunite with my wildish part, my true spirit and the soul of who I really am.

And I know that each of you reading this book has had something you have also hidden, something that if and when you let it out of hiding, will actually make you stand out and be seen, not only in a positive way, but in a way that is uniquely you. It will give you permission to open your voice.

Regardless of your age now, eventually you will face the same issues I just shared: how to be ok with being who you are when you are no longer a saucy young chick, and how to still be seen as a visible, alive entrepreneur. Some women face this when they turn 40. It really isn't about your age; it's your state of mind.

You can begin right now to accept yourself the way you are and stand fully in that place that says, "I can and am building a business and life path based on my values, my true spirit and my voice in the world." And you can be highly successful at it.

- How does your Wild Woman express herself?
- What is she telling you to do?
- How can you bring her out of hiding more?

STEP 3: BEING AUTHENTIC

I believe the traditional way of doing business is damaging to many women because as women, we do business the way we do everything. It doesn't work for us to suddenly step into another identity while at work. This is a good thing because, in today's world, people want authenticity. I love that word and it's one of this decade's most meaningful 'it' words. Why is that? Because we have all been bombarded with corporate messaging that is anything but real, and now we are sick of hype and marketing that lies and manipulates.

Indeed, the best marketing is about you being YOU. Who you are is way more important than what you do. **Regardless of how large your business is, people want to connect with you, the real you, your spirit part of you; the woman who dances, screams, sobs, digs in the garden or whatever.** It's all about your story, your challenges and what makes your light shine. That's what draws people to you like bees to honey. People are starved for real relationships and this is what business is all about.

Women tend to have a strong intuition and heart-centeredness that, when they tap into it, becomes a wellspring of creative energy and inspiration that can be carried into their messages and innovative ideas. But many are still influenced by a strong picture of what they have to do and be, in order to be successful.

One of my clients, Susan, who is an energy healer, shared the pain she felt about having to spend hours in front of her computer on social media trying to sell herself. Her posts were very promotional and 'salesy.' She hated this and felt it drained her life force.

Susan kept overlooking the fact that she could incorporate her real healing energy into her marketing and Facebook posts, and that voice would in fact speak to her readers. As with many of us, the two parts of herself were separated. On one hand, there was the lovely deep work she did with her clients where she is 100% with them, giving empathy and connecting to a deep place. And yet her marketing messages were all heady, with no hint of her true heart and soul. She was trying to put her round shape into a square box and not only did it not work, she was feeling stressed and out of balance.

Now, when I begin to feel stress in my business, I step away from the work and take a walk to get back to myself, my real self including my intuition and heart, and I can feel my energy return. Like many things, it is a practice in itself to stay in this place, but this is the natural place for women so you will be much more productive and balanced when you operate this way.

In this way, you begin to realize it's not all about you; it's also about global change and knowing that these values are what the world needs right now. If you are working in a job or for an organization that does not see who you really are and fails to look deeper into what you see with your insight and want to bring forth, you will feel this separation deep in your soul, which will begin to feel like a garden without water or nutrients. The only way for you to continue to be in your job is to shut off your true nature. As a result, you fail to thrive and the company you work for also misses the most valuable offerings that you could bring.

As a leader of your own business you have the deep opportunity to step into this partnership fully, to build your business based on these values and to recognize that both your Wise Woman and your Wild Woman are with you everyday. All you have to do is call, ask for help and be open to their ideas and points of view, and then listen.

- ◉ How do you show your authentic self everyday?
- ◉ What does being authentic mean to you?
- ◉ What parts of your authentic self have you been holding back?

Inviting Your Wise and Wild Woman

Closing your eyes, imagine you are sitting around a fire in community with your soul sisters, a group of smart, heart-centered visionary women. Look around the circle and see other women who are doing their work in the world while staying aligned with their feminine truth.

Breathe in the smells and tune into your real wisdom, what you know you are meant to do and how you want to be living and working.

Invite both your Wise and Wild Women to join you. They are two aspects of your true soul partner and may appear as one image or two. Wise Woman is the one who holds your deep wisdom and inner knowing, while Wild Woman is your free spirit and wild feminine nature.

Do this in your own way, but make the invitation clear and welcoming.

You may see an image of someone or you might just have a feeling of her presence. You might experience her appearing but then discount it as being just your imagination. That's fine; imagination is part of intuition and it is real. Being your partner, she might just show up via your imagination!

Ask her to share her wisdom with you about where you are going, what you need to do next and how you need to shift. Just listen and be open even if you don't understand.

Write everything you heard in your circle. It could be words, sentences or colors.

Find a woman in your own circle who you can share this with. Sharing will take you to a deeper level of understanding.

Would you like a deeper audio version of this visualization?
Go to: WiserandWilder.com/resources

Circle Power

"Throughout my entrepreneurial journey I've learned hard lessons about where and how to find my tribe, my circle, my people. A few years ago I decided, once again, to join a women's networking group. At first I loved the energy and the connections made. I wasn't there to find clients — I'd already learned that didn't work for my particular business — instead I was looking for community and support for my very big dreams.

I went to a local event with the CEO of this organization and fell pray to the sales pitch for the annual conference. My gut told me not to sign up, but my head/ego wanted to be part of what everyone else was excited about. I decided to be a vendor to promote my book, thinking these were my people, so it would be a great success. I paid for the conference, the pricey hotel, meals and flights—and I knew as soon as we arrived that I'd made a big mistake.

The whole conference was about pushing products, like coaching programs that cost up to $30,000. Break out sessions were pitch fests and I was disheartened and mad. I was there to talk with women about getting into alignment with their relationship with money while all around me people were committing tens of thousands of credit card dollars to programs they couldn't afford. Intuitively, I knew I was in the wrong circle and that I didn't want to do business this way, but I kept telling myself that there must be something wrong with me.

When I got back from the conference I had a conversation with my business manager. She reminded me of how I had clearly stated that I wanted to focus on doing what is right for me, not what might be right for other people. I looked at my numbers for the quarter and, sure enough, the financial impact of trying to make myself at home in a circle of people that didn't resonate was a very expensive and important lesson.

The most important circle to honor is your own. This is what I continue to learn, even after 14 years of being in business. When I stand solidly in what I know and trust myself to listen deeply to spirit, I'm more likely to choose situations and people that align. Self-doubt is toxic, yet so is the inability to forgive ourselves when we make mistakes. My intention is to surround myself with circles of people that elevate and accept me while calling on my creativity, love and kindness; circles that celebrate my successes and hold me when I falter; where we serve spirit in the deepest way possible."

~Luna Jaffe

I know women, lots of women, like Luna who have made the mistake of choosing the wrong group to be a part of. All too many include spending a small fortune on high level coaching programs that promise high profits. Many of these women are new to their businesses and therefore vulnerable. They believe that if they follow the steps laid out by these programs, they will automatically get the six or seven figure income that's promised.

When Luna realized she was in the wrong group, she quickly took some steps to protect herself: "I am very susceptible to high-powered quick sales pitches promising high profits, so that's how I ended up there. I'm a sucker for that stuff, but now I know when I get those calls, I just have to hang up the phone."

These schemes can be quite alluring, especially for new business owners or entrepreneurs who primarily work alone. They want to belong, to receive guidance and to be part of a group. Many times this is because they haven't learned to trust their own intuition or inner knowing, and they are afraid if they don't sign-up right then, they will miss the opportunity and be left out. Does this sound familiar?

Like Luna, you might have found yourself trusting someone else's model of business without realizing you were walking into a box. This chapter is about saying no to other people's boxes and instead creating your own authentic circle, one that reflects your business model and will provide the ongoing support you need.

Circle Energy

Circles feel good. Next time you're at the beach, take a stick and draw a circle around you. Then stand in the middle. How does it feel? One woman told me the circle felt like a force field that would keep her safe. Another woman said it made her feel special, like she was in the center of her world. Still another said she felt like she could create anything within that space. We did this at a workshop I ran recently and every woman there felt more empowered, energized and centered once she put herself into a circle.

I also had them draw a square and notice how they felt standing in the center. One woman said it felt like she had boundaries she couldn't cross, while another said she felt diminished or smaller. A third woman said it felt like there were rules to follow.

By its very nature, a circle has life force; it shines and is open and inviting. The circle symbol is perfect for women whose natures are naturally wholistic. Women are round beings and choosing to create your own circle will unconsciously remind you of your tribal connections, sitting around a fire with your tribe. It represents your home, your warm hearth and your people.

Tapping into circle energy is an important part of nurturing and growing the kind of energy you want for your life force, which in turn will help you create the kind of support and expansiveness that will help you to shine and grow your dream business.

Circles are found everywhere in nature. Flowers, spider webs, ripples on a pond, the sun, the full moon, mandarin oranges or pearls, to name a few. Begin looking and you can add many more to the list.

I can't think of one square shape that is not human-made. People create boxes and when you are in one you know it. A box with its walls and corners can feel confining. There is nowhere to go and it can feel like you are bouncing from one wall to another.

A box often represents the conventional or "right" way of being. When it's based on someone else's values and culture, as is often the case, you can end up feeling boxed in, stifled and disconnected.

You might join something, hoping it's going to be your circle and then you realize it's just another box that's not you; it's not where your Wise and Wild woman is going to thrive. Many women, like Luna, have found themselves trying to fit into a box they had hoped would be a circle.

A box can also be somewhere to go if you want to hide and not be seen. Maybe you don't know who you really are yet, or perhaps you do know but do not trust your feminine wisdom. When this happens, many women try to mold themselves into being square shapes in order to fit in.

By contrast, your circle feels open, not confined, and can easily overlap with other circles for collaboration that brings in more depth, perspectives, sharing and connections, which is just what you want and need.

It's important to get it deep in your soul that you need to run your business the Woman's Way. This includes both being in circles with your tribe and bringing circle energy into all of your business activities.

Circle is a state of mind. It is a BEINGness that is similar to how you feel when you are chanting, looking at the sunset, participating in a ritual, singing, laying in the bathtub or whatever else makes you feel right and connected to source.

Circle is a State of Mind

That BEINGness is you. At a workshop, I asked all the women to walk barefoot in the wet sand. Then we stood in a circle facing inward where we could see our footsteps. Each of our footprints was distinct and perfect. When we looked closely, we realized each one was slightly different. The way one person stood made the sole deeper, while the way another person stood made her toes very faint. When we tried to place our own feet in another person's prints, we saw that it was impossible to stand exactly in someone else's footprint. We realized that each of us had a distinct place in the circle.

You may not have words to describe the BEINGness that you bring to the circle, but you know it's your way, and when you find a circle where your footprints belong, you know you are with your people. You know that what you bring to the whole is needed because it calls on your greatest gifts and allows you to engage in ways that bring out the best in you.

Osho describes this so well in the Participation Card in his Tarot deck:

> The mandala has a quality like that energy field that forms around a Buddha, where all the individuals taking part in the circle make a unique contribution to create a unified and vital whole. It is like a flower whose wholeness is even more beautiful than the sum of its parts, at the same time enhancing the beauty of each individual petal.

Circle energy allows us to create something bigger than ourselves and make a difference in the world in a way that is so much more powerful than if we tried to do it alone.

How to Tune into Circle Energy

Maybe you are thinking that you need to be meditating, walking on the beach or attending a workshop with others in order to step into this mindset, but the most lovely thing about a mindset is that it is available anywhere and anytime. It can exist in many contexts and can be created in any situation, such as online, in a coffee shop or on the telephone.

It is a way of being and an inner attitude that becomes a new way of being once you practice it. It simply involves being authentically you and doesn't require you to be in a quiet place, with the right kind of music and a candle lit. Those things are lovely and can help to remind you, but you can feel this way on a noisy subway or in an airport.

I think the true power of feminine leadership comes from showing up 100% and being present with each other in circles. A circle can be just two women, it can include men who are part of your tribe or it can be online in Facebook groups. It can even be present in yourself when you are alone in your office because you carry the awareness that you are never alone. There are always others who will understand, plus your Wise Woman is always with you.

I've had some women tell me they want their business to thrive but they can't do social media because it feels too superficial and chaotic, plus they regard it as a waste of time. Part of being in your circle means being open and involved. If you are centered and in the zone, Facebook can be part of your circle. I've experienced this over and over with Facebook posts. One phenomenal thing about social media is that it allows you to expand your circle to include people you previously could barely conceive of knowing and connecting with.

Recently I posted this sharing on my timeline:

> Part of being me is that I feel stuff deeply and I can't ignore it. It keeps me up at night, affects my gut, my energy, everything. So I have to dig in and face it. I write, paint, walk and get out in nature. As a result, such a deep insight surfaces. The good thing about being my age is that the awareness and awakenings come faster and faster. I have just survived one of these times recently - a painful process of birthing into the light, but now I SEE. Who else gets this?? I would love to know how this works for you.

Within hours, I had 60 plus likes and over 40 comments from people sharing how it is for them and offering support tools, books and so much presence. I felt blessed and in deep connection with everyone.

With Facebook, I only see a circle. However, it can be a box if you aren't mindful. Again, you have to decide where you want to be and who you want to be with. All those people who responded became part of my circle and joined me for that bit of time. That is a huge gift and so heart warming. I felt seen, heard and cared for on that one day, more than many people feel in a whole year. Plus, I was able to share something authentically transparent with them. Since I want to be seen and stand out, that felt good. I had to be real, though. Can you see that? If I had made something up just to do marketing, I would have moved into box energy and I wouldn't have gotten as many valuable authentic comments.

Are you getting why I love circles?

I especially love mandarin oranges. Not only do they taste yummy, but also my favorite part is peeling off the rind, which comes off so easily, and seeing all the sections perfectly fitted together to form a lovely circle brought to me by Mother Earth.

I tend to create all my teaching tools using mandalas and pie charts, my version of two-dimensional oranges. It's easy to stand back, see the whole picture and also see the pie pieces and how each one relates to all the others. There is no form that is more powerful for women.

I've developed tools to help me understand marketing and business planning and it was through the process of beginning with a circle and using colored pencils to create pie pieces that it all began to make sense to me. I had read hundreds of business books and I didn't get it until I made my own illustrations using circle energy. Of course I then shared these tools with my clients and witnessed women lighting up and beginning to get it for the first time.

Women need to see the whole picture. It is the most powerful way to begin to create a business plan or a new project, or solve a problem. Mind mapping with a circle is excellent for women because it's very natural and wholistic. When I do mind mapping, I usually begin with a large piece of paper and create a large circle in the middle before anything. Any rectanglular shaped paper will have those pesky corners that you want to avoid.

Getting Out of the Box

Many creativity trainings these days talk about 'getting out of the box.' This whole idea can be scary to some people who want to be safe. If you are in a box, it can feel secure. You are confined in a box that's actually limiting or conventional, but it's what you know. I have had countless conversations with women who needed help but were too scared to come out of their safe box even though it wasn't supporting them to grow. I always let them know that they can find safety in a circle too.

Getting out of a box can bring up fears of looking like a fool, making mistakes and experiencing failures, all that scary stuff. These feelings are represented by the archetypal fool in the Tarot and can feel like leaping into the unknown. However, it can also feel exhilarating to finally make a decision and take a risk.

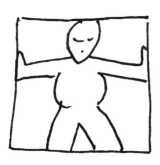

Where a box has corners with no escape, a circle is open and flowing. Circles imply sitting together, listening, getting support and connecting. Women tend to learn from each other because we all have the potential to tap into our strong intuition and heart-centeredness and when we do so, a wellspring of creative energy and inspiration arises which we can convert into our messages and innovative ideas.

Now when I think circle, I immediately feel safe and surrounded by people who I trust. I know I will be supported, listened to, heard and more. But for people who are just learning about how to step out of that box and create a circle environment for themselves, how can they know what it will feel like when they get there? Here's what to look for to begin piecing your circle together.

What Does Your Circle Look Like?

Your own circle is a reflection of what it really means for you to be authentic. It includes everything that is you, even if you're not sure how it relates to your business.

Not only is this an amazing personal process, it will also help you with your marketing. In this day and age, you need to stand out and know what makes you attractive. Part of what attracts people to you is going to be found inside your circle. You might not realize it until you create your circle and fill it with all that you are, but then it will almost magically stand out!

Creating your own visionary circle is a powerful process as you can see in this example below.

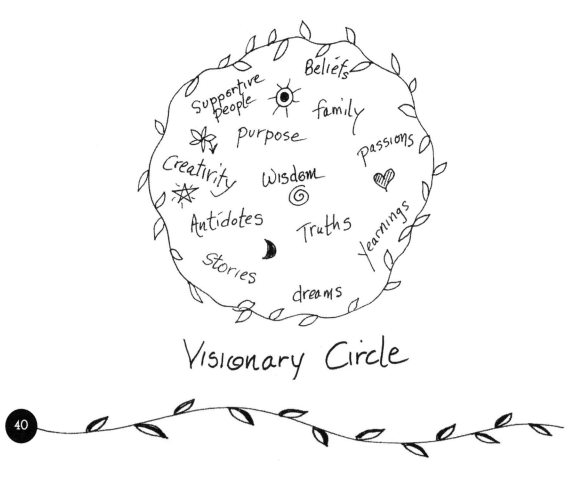

Visionary Circle

I once did this with another group on a beach. Everyone made a circle and filled it with things that represented what felt good to them. Even though the beach was covered with just rocks, sticks and seaweed, everyone's circle looked completely different. Each woman then told her story that was all contained in her powerful circle.

Your story will actually help you to create your circle as well. Stories are traditionally shared in circles so it can hold that circle energy of who you are. Your stories are rich and can explain where you come from, where you've been and who you are better than any other kind of narrative. No one has the same story. Your story is totally unique and it can't be copied. This is why it's so powerful in marketing. People want to know you - the real you.

My Circle Story

I began doodling when I was old enough to hold a pencil. I loved to draw anything. I'm the kind of person who can't sit in a meeting without doodling. My notes from college lectures were filled with doodles in the margins. Compared to other people's notes, they looked messy and I never wanted anyone to see what I was doing. I now know that I'm a kinesthetic type who needs to touch and move, but I didn't know that then.

In elementary school, my teachers told me to pay attention and they took my doodling pencils away from me. I thought that meant I wasn't doing school right. I thought doodling was a negative trait so I starting hiding it.

Some years ago, I found some of my doodles and drawings stored in a box in my mom's basement. What I saw amazed me; page after page, my drawings were filled with circle images. Then I remembered how my earliest doodles always began with circles. When I got a little older, around five or six, I began drawing figures of girls sitting together in circles. There they were, scads of them drawn on the backs of mimeograph paper my dad brought home from his office. Looking at these drawings I got the chills. At age five, I already knew something on a non-verbal level, something so profound and important that I was bringing it into form in my scribbles.

The inner message from my drawings became lost as I moved into being a teenager. I didn't trust the feminine part of myself or understand her. A boy bullied me and my girlfriends never stood up for me, which confused me because I just wanted to fit in and be accepted.

What I was expressing in those drawings from my early years was a yearning for community with other females to sit together. My spirit was putting out what I needed to manifest in my life, but I didn't get the message.

Then, in my early 30s, I went to a therapist because I was getting migraines. She helped me unearth this part of me that I had forgotten, telling me I needed to find women and connect with my own inner feminine. I had no idea what that was, but it rang true and it re-ignited that core part of me. I began to put out antennas and developed some deep connections with women. I felt like these people saw the real me. My migraines stopped and never came back.

Later, I was part of hosting women's gatherings in New Zealand where we sat in circles, just like in my five-year-old drawings. I have never felt more at home. We often had a fire in the center that we kept burning for an entire week. We began each circle with singing, ritual and eye gazing, all that New Age stuff that fed my soul, and I felt my roots growing into the soil of Mother Earth.

Every gathering was a profound experience with women showing up, opening their hearts and souls and burning their past pain into the fire.

Together, we recreated women's community for all of our benefit and for the benefit of the whole world. We knew we were making profound changes at a core level so we each could leave at the end of the week taking what we had found out to our corners of the universe.

The corporate version of this is called Leadership Training, but that term doesn't even begin to touch what we did. In truth, we were developing ourselves as leaders in a big way. We were changing our souls, our spirits and ourselves. We were doing what only a group of women with intention to shift at our deepest levels can do in a circle.

Twenty years later I was part of a circle called Women of the 14th Moon, a ceremonial gathering of women, and we still sat in a circle with a fire in the center. It is so important for our empowerment, healing and opening our voices. Every woman leaves the weekend feeling the power of the circle and the transformations inside.

Finding Your Unique Circle Power

Maybe, like many women who started a business from a skill or a passion, you ended up all alone in your little office, not on a beach or around a fire. As women, we are not wired to operate this way! We need community. I am a solo entrepreneur with a home office so I go to a teahouse in my neighborhood and spend the day working there because I like being surrounded by others doing the same thing.

How can you find your circle? You will never find it in a box, whether that be your office or even your own psyche. Your circle is where your own Wise and Wild Woman lives with you and you will need to step out of your box to connect with her. How you do that will be your own unique path.

My circle includes going on walks, being in the forest or near the ocean, or riding my bike, because these things help me to keep my clay centered on the wheel. When my clay begins to feel wobbly, those things serve as antidotes for stress, worry and confusion. They take me back to a place of center.

You might want to try physically sitting with other women in a circle. I don't know about you, but that immediately makes me feel like I can grow and become who I'm meant to be. Your circle could open up and become a dance floor, a canvas or a large clay bowl. It could be a long red ribbon winding around your tribe, or a knitted scarf a hundred feet long reaching back to your ancestors. Or you might prefer being in a cyber circle with committed women connecting online.

How will you know when you have found your circle? When you are standing fully in your circle, you will be more intuitive and have more inner sight. You will find solutions to problems easily, whip out blog posts and gain more clarity about your marketing plan. You'll know whom you want to connect or collaborate with and how to use your voice.

And that circle can just be your beginning. Like a mandarin orange, your circle can have sections from which you create new circles. It can go deeper and deeper like those little Russian dolls that fit inside of each other.

How to Stay in Your Visionary Circle

SAY NO TO SABOTAGERS

Certain things are all deadly for visionaries because they will make you forget who you are and what you came here to do (your dharma). They will dry up your creativity and passion and might make you feel like you don't have one unique thought in your head. You will doubt whether you have anything to teach anyone. In that moment, you won't remember that you are part of a larger community of people who support you. You'll forget your purpose. It's like having the worst case of amnesia.

Worry, fear, self-doubt   Fatigue
Comparing yourself to others   Lack of support
Over-working   Blaming
Poor nutrition   Addictions

Outside of your circle, you will struggle and forget who you are: A visionary with a gift that needs to be given to the world.

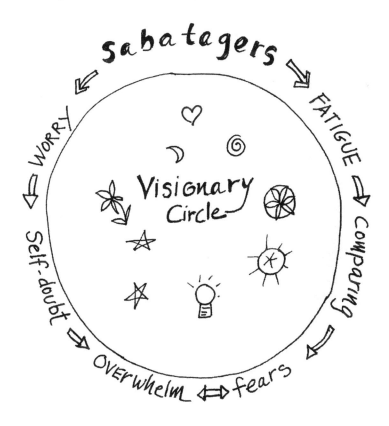

Say Yes to Your Circle Power

One important characteristic of any visionary woman is that she knows she isn't ordinary. If you try to be ordinary or normal, you will walk out of your circle. Dancers and figure skaters often talk about tuning into to their chi energy spot before performing. This enables them to be centered and tuned in. Only from that place will they be able to stay balanced, float through their routine and be the best they can be. They will be anything but ordinary. Instead, they will be magnificent, unique and one of a kind because they are fully in the center of their circle. If they begin doubting, fretting or worrying, they are instantly out of that space and more likely to trip and fall.

If you have ever seen the bright full moon in the dark sky, you will notice that halo of light surrounding it. When you are inside your circle, you also have that energy surrounding you, and any work you do from that place will shine and be aligned.

Inside your circle are antidotes (your medicines) for everything on this list and the tools to transform or transmute each of them into intuitive awarenesses that will make your genius blossom.

Your Visionary Circle

Your own Visionary Circle is a footprint of who you really are in your quirky, distinctive way. At those times when you lose the thread, your footprint will be there to remind you and help you to find the thread again, so you can carry on weaving your vision.

Your circle can include:

Who you are	Your stories
What makes you unique	Your beliefs
The larger picture of yourself	Your fears
Creativity	Your passions
Wisdom	Your missions
Self-talk	Your yearnings
Your support people	
Your family	

Grab some paper and markers or colored pens and try this process.

STEP ONE
Find a place that is inspirational to you and will help you connect with your soul; where your Wild and Wise Woman is at home.

STEP TWO
State your intention. I, (your name) am a visionary woman and this is my circle that supports my genius. Draw a circle on a large sheet of paper. Don't worry about it being symmetrical; it won't be and that's fine.

STEP THREE
Invite your Wise and Wild Women to be with you. Call in any other support you want to help you with the process.

STEP FOUR

Divide your circle into five sections. Again, don't worry about making it perfect; there is no right or wrong way. Label each section using the words below. There are so many variations on how you could do this, such as collecting small stones and writing each word on a stone. Feel free to use what is around you or what you have on hand.

- ◉ Dharma - Inherent abilities
- ◉ Community - Supportive people
- ◉ Purpose - Vision for yourself
- ◉ Passion - What excites you
- ◉ Medicines - What you need

STEP FIVE

You can begin anywhere in the circle as there is actually no order. Tune into the energy of that section and go into a place of mindfulness. Imagine you are standing in the center of your circle. From that place, write or draw any words, colors or symbols that emerge.

STEP SIX

Continue until you have filled in all five areas. Light a small candle in the center so your circle becomes your fire circle and the center of your light and power. Give thanks.

STEP SEVEN

Keep this on your altar as a reminder, share it with your mastermind group and add new words to it anytime.

Say these words: "I am a visionary and I am meant to follow my soulful path."

Go to WiserandWilder.com/resources to download a template of this and read more about how to do this same process on the beach.

Success Portal

After I decided to be a life coach, I quit my job and I wanted to begin getting clients right away. I had spent hours and hours developing programs that I knew were good and I was excited about my offerings. I just needed clients.

I contacted a coach to help me and told her I wanted to get to $3,000 month within three months and if she could help me do that, I would hire her. She told me that not only could she not guarantee that, but also it was very unlikely to happen. She said a lot depended on me and how much I might get stuck in my own issues. I didn't think I had any issues other than needing clients to hire me, and I was going to get help with that by hiring a marketing and business coach to give me those skills. In the end, I decided to hire her anyway because I liked her honesty, but in truth, I still had my agenda.

I am embarrassed to share that I ended up fighting with her on every phone call. It felt like she was suggesting I do stuff that was going to take way too long, such as getting proof that my programs would work. She told me to write blog posts with tips and then gave me feedback that they were too 'salsey.' I was trying to sell but she said it was too soon and I would push people away, but I needed money.

Now I get where she was coming from, but at the time I was horrible and argumentative. I had no idea what I would have to do to get clients and when she led me down that path, I criticized her for not giving me what I paid her for. I am so ashamed that I am not willing to put my name on this story, but I do want to share it because I am sure I am not the only one who has felt this way. I had to go to rock bottom, get a part time job, and in the end it took a year before I had even one client. By then I had learned so much about how to start a coaching business and even more about myself.

~Rachel

Rachel's story is just one version of stories I've heard from hundreds of my clients who started a business based on their expertise and vision. Thinking they were going to make money right away, they were shocked when they realized they were going to have to face many personal issues first. Like Rachel, they were surprised at how long it would take and the difficulties they would confront doing all the business parts, but eventually, they all had to face their own issues first and foremost.

In this chapter, I will share the Visionary-Entrepreneur Picture I created to help people understand that just having a vision and desire won't create financial success or any other kind. However, once you understand this picture, the path comes into view and the transformation begins.

What is a Visionary Entrepreneur?

In order to develop any kind of successful business, you need to have a vision of where you want to go, plus a map with steps for how to get there. However, visionaries are in a special group of people who don't always begin this way. Maybe you are wondering if you are one.

Here are three main things that help define who a visionary entrepreneur is. As you will see, it isn't always so black and white.

World Changer. As a true visionary entrepreneur, your passion is to deeply make a difference in the world and have a desire for real change. Your vision is way bigger than your business and can include social change that reflects the profound reason for doing your work.

Personal Visionary. You not only want to make a significant difference but you also want to feel personally fulfilled in what you do. It's important that you are doing exactly what your heart and soul is meant to express in this lifetime. In this regard, you are following your own unique vision, which overflows and overlaps into your business. As a visionary entrepreneur, you are actualizing your life purpose via your business.

Innovative and Creative. You look at things in unique ways and are willing to take risks and do what's not been done before. Some of your ideas might not seem to fly financially, so it can be about overcoming huge obstacles and looking at how to make it all work. You choose to hang around with a tribe who is similar to you and won't try to hold you back.

Visionary entrepreneurs must learn how to merge all of these elements plus their creativity and passion with their entrepreneurial side.

Some people not only have the qualities listed here but also an MBA, money to invest or investors and a business plan. They are fortunate for sure, but even then, building a successful business will still be hard work. That's just the way it is!

Most of the women in my tribe are operating on an opposite paradigm. They often have little or no money to invest and no business skills. These visionaries don't want to compartmentalize their lives; they want their passion to be their work and they want it to support their dreams as well.

What Kind of Visionary Are You?

Maybe you no longer can handle your job. It feels like it is sucking your life force and your soul is lost in a work situation that doesn't allow your real gifts to shine.

 You might also be someone like I was who never went the job route. I knew very early on that I wasn't cut out for that lifestyle. The only real jobs I had were part-time and even then, it was very hard because I was working only for the money to support my real passion.

You may be someone who knows your vision - it's what you are meant to do - and yet you never really wanted to own a business and that's the part that becomes the real challenge. This is the story for many artists and other creative types; they only want to do their art and resent the time it takes to do the business part.

But, in fact, for the first few years in your seedling business, you will need to be spending more time on marketing and planning than on doing the visionary work you love. So in those early years, you might encounter feeling ambivalent about what you must do, like you have one foot in and one foot out.

It can be like starting to plant a garden in the spring because you can envision the beautiful plants and eating the fresh veggies come summer, but then forgetting to water it, or not getting around to fertilizing or pulling the weeds and expecting the plants to grow. When they don't grow bountifully and some of them even die, you feel discouraged and wonder if the seeds you planted were bad. The thought crosses your mind that you might have had something to do with it, but you don't dwell on that.

Sound familiar? This was me 100%, so I know the challenges of choosing to grow a visionary business but not wanting to learn the new habits of tending the garden. I thought it took too much time, I didn't understand how to do it and I didn't enjoy it. But at the same time, I wanted the success and cash flow.

Or you might be one of those people who, after a couple years of a pathetic garden, finally got your hands in the soil and did enough to have some success. Now you want to build a larger garden that includes fussier plants that need more tending. All of your issues re-surface, including self-doubt and questioning, and you realize these issues aren't going away.

You wanted to do the thing you love, whether it's coaching, painting, designing, healing, writing or whatever. Like most visionaries, you can see the big picture of where you want to be. You can see yourself speaking to hundreds of people on a stage, writing books that inspire thousands of people or building a health center that you've dreamed about for years and years. But it feels like you have to cross a gulf as large as the Grand Canyon to just get to the place where you can do your work and be prosperous.

When it feels like your real vision is years away from manifesting, you get discouraged. What you haven't realized is that the real growth is always right in this moment. It happens as you discover the creativity involved with the business part you have been avoiding.

The Three-Part Portal

My Visionary Entrepreneur Picture involves three pieces of the process of being on a soulful path. If you want to not just be a visionary, but also grow a successful business, you have to be willing to delve into this process.

Notice how where the visionary and the entrepreneur circles overlap, it creates an almond shaped portal sometimes called the Vesica Pisces. This represents the third essential portal of growth and transformation and is also considered a universal symbol of the feminine. It can be regarded as the doorway to real creation. I am not an expert at Sacred Geometry, but I know this symbol has been used over and over for hundreds of years. It's the design on the well cover of the Sacred Chalice Well at Glastonbury.

When I designed this picture, I didn't know this would happen. I just wanted to find a way to illustrate my teaching, but this emerged and it is so powerful. Remember, part of my mission is to help women to save the world, so I want you to really get this process.

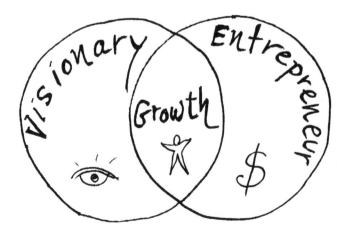

Imagine yourself in each area and see if you can relate.

Your visionary wants to:
- Do what you love
- Make a world-changing difference
- Follow your passion
- Do things your own way
- Express your soul work
- Feel alive and connected
- Be in a circle with other visionaries
- Help people
- Vision, heal, create, initiate

Your entrepreneur wants to:
- Be paid well and have strong cash flow
- Follow the steps to growing a strong business
- Identify as a businesswoman
- Be an excellent money manager
- Make responsible decisions
- Have goals and plans
- Be disciplined and committed, step in fully
- Be in a circle with successful business owners
- Lead, succeed, manage

Your personal growth wants to:
- Bring these two together
- Dig deep into your emotions and heal your old story
- Grow yourself spiritually and do your soul work
- Acknowledge what triggers your fears
- Face this part of yourself without reacting
- Turn your emotions into inner sight and intuition
- Let go of what's not working
- Develop new habits
- Be in a circle with people who are authentic and open
- Step into self-actualization
- Shift, grow, feel, transform

In order to manifest your vision and create a successful business, you need to activate all three of these areas. Although this process offers a transformative doorway, many people avoid it, skip steps or just hope for instant self-actualization. It doesn't work that way. I've been involved in personal growth for over 35 years and nothing has made me face my stuff as much as owning a business. Every time, it takes me closer to my real issues before I can move closer to success.

Here is another metaphor that might make sense to you. Ignoring one of these parts will feel like sitting on a three-legged stool with one of its legs missing. Historically, we as women know stools. It's where we sat to milk cows, spin wool, tend the fire and shell peas, right? All three legs are necessary to provide solid support so we can do our work. In the same way, all three of these areas must be nurtured and kept alive in order for you to be fully supported.

We can all understand these simple ideas and images, but it's actually not easy to keep your stool balanced so you maintain a strong foundation. Here are some ways you might get sidetracked in your process and get stuck in one side or the other, unable to access your portal to success.

The Seduction of the Visionary

Many who make the entrepreneurial choice do not fully embrace all three areas immediately. For most women, your initial comfort level is in your visionary circle, so this is where you put 90 percent of your energy. This is where your passion lives so it's seductive. Then you wonder why you are struggling to make your businesses work.

Over-focusing on your visionary circle can remain unconscious, so you don't realize you are looking at things through a filter. You believe you are working hard, but actually you are refusing to focus on certain areas because you are concerned that they could cause you to lose your free spirit or your visions. Running the business end of things feels like walking into a box and you want to avoid that.

Ironically, you might be working hard at avoiding that box, and yet by your very avoidance you end up feeling stuck in a different box.

INDECISION

The first box is indecision. You might not be sure who you really are yet, so you feel unsure of fully making the commitment to plant your garden and say, "Yes, I am going to grow this as a business." The question looms: 'What is my life purpose and what am I meant to do?'

In your quest for a purposeful answer, you want to be 100% sure that this is your correct life path, so you spend all your time reading The Course in Miracles or other insightful books to help you become clearer abut your direction.

This kind of thinking can in itself be a trap or a box because you might never have an absolute answer. Feeling purposeful and passionate is a process, not a destination. **Often, choosing to grow a business will be like following a thread and you won't necessarily know where that thread will take you.** It could end up being your pivotal life work or maybe not.

I find that, most often, it's women in their 30s who face this trap. Right after their Saturn return (an astrological time of becoming a grown-up), they feel they are ready to stand solidly and be an adult and do what they are meant to do in the world. The problem is they might only have a glimpse of a feeling and a decade later they will download another whole new awareness about who they are and what they are meant to do.

If this is you, trust in following your thread because that is the key to allowing the magic of personal growth and self-development to help you grow in ways you couldn't even imagine. Everything you do now will morph into what you will do next. As an older woman who has been through it, I empathize and promise.

In my case, I got my BFA when I was 22 and had no idea what I would do with it. Then I had a seven-year pottery business that lasted until I was 32. Over the next three years, I got my Masters in counseling. For the next 15 years, I was a therapist and I learned to listen and help women transform, grow inside and become more alive in their spirits. Fast forward to today and I find that these are all things I now do in my present business, and there are still more horizons: At age of 68, I am becoming a painter, something I was never good at until this year!

My Wise and Wild Woman had her own way of making it all work.

Fear of Losing Your Spirit

Another box that keeps some women stuck in the visionary circle are fears they developed in childhood. Some have clear memories about losing their free spirits and feel grief or rage about it.

I had one client who shared that in her Catholic school experience as a child the nuns taught them to 'not show off,' which meant not revealing their light, and basically try to remain unseen. I remember another woman telling me she was whipped for dancing erotically and this was mixed up with being sexually abused. She learned to hide herself completely. With childhood memories like these, women will often hold onto their spirit for dear life. They have a body memory of what it felt like to be cut off from their wildness because they were told those feelings and ways of being were wrong or not an acceptable way for girls to be.

If this is your story, possibly after a lot of personal growth or therapy you were able to reclaim your spirit and now you are hyper sensitive about losing her again. You're afraid of being boxed into things that make you feel less free, like running a business. As a result, you keep your energy in the visionary circle, hanging on for dear life. You think you are running a business, but you are not really doing it 100%. You ignore the stuff you don't like because it drains your spirit. You might not realize that you actually have the opportunity to live in the now and re-write your story.

FEELING DISABLED

Visionary box number three is the trapped feeling you get when stuff feels hard and you think you aren't smart enough. This was my box. Based on messages from my childhood, I was sure I wasn't smart enough to understand financial stuff so I avoided it. Of course this affected my business growth and my ability to manage my money. What finally motivated me to shift this was realizing that my Wild Woman would actually be way freer and have so many more opportunities to express herself if I could get the financial piece under control. Can you see how this transformation piece is so important?

Some of these issues are deep seated and it's easy to forget that they are only a story and not an absolute truth. You try to push them aside but it doesn't work to ignore them because if you focus on only being the visionary, you won't be able to grow a real business that will sustain itself and you.

The Overwhelm of the Entrepreneur

Once you wake up to the fact that to run a successful business means doing the business parts fully, you kneel down, get your hands in the soil and realize how much you don't know. Most visionaries have no business background so the challenges are greater and require learning while doing. Even for those who do have a business background, more often than not it was focused on a different business model than what you need now to grow your visionary garden.

Unrealistic Expectations

Many of us have the expectation that we can open our business and have money coming in right away. Once that doesn't happen and you decide to get help, you discover how much work you have to do to grow healthy roots before your garden can grow lush and thrive.

Desperation

From a place of desperation, you might jump a 100% into the entrepreneurial circle, but then you become so separated from your original vision that you soon begin to feel dried up and depleted. You forget who you are and why you started your business to begin with. You become driven and sacrifice everything: time, money, family and health. Before long, you become Depleted Woman and then Dried up Woman from working 24/7 and losing yourself in the process.

This has happened to me. I felt so determined to get my business working and to do everything to make it successful that I put on blinders. Not only did I get sick, but I also experienced the joy in my life gradually seeping away. My stress and worry increased until I realized I was cut off completely from the wildish part of myself.

Now I listen sharply and trust my instincts. If I wake up in the morning and know I need to be walking on the beach, I listen and take heed. I get myself to the beach and with my feet in the sand, I feel my spirit self return and start getting glimpses of the joyful reasons for being alive. Then, when I get back to my business, I am able to do things in a more grounded and balanced way, with all three legs of my stool holding me up.

A few years ago, a quote took hold that is still prominent on social media: "Follow your bliss and the money will come." It is true that if you don't follow your bliss, you might have misery, a job of drudgery and feel cut-off from your wildish self. However, even if you begin your business from the place of following a blissful vision, you may also find misery if you aren't awake and aware of how you are avoiding fully stepping into being a business woman. On the other hand, you must remain aware of becoming a type A and ending up depleted. Either way, the process of staying balanced involves transformation, personal-growth and self-actualization. You can't avoid the middle portal, that almond in the middle, which represents the doorway to transformation and growth

Empowerment through the Personal Growth Portal

I have had the experience of falling into both of the traps discussed above. Focusing too much energy on my vision kept me struggling financially so I wasn't able to fully do my work in the world. Then I flipped the other way and became overly focused on developing my business and I felt exhausted and forgot why I was even doing it. I didn't always know it at the time, but whenever I got out of balance, I needed to turn to my own personal growth Wise Woman.

SPIRITUAL PRACTICE

Now I know that running a solo business is always a spiritual practice, all of the time. Like any practice, it requires maintenance, which for me means: breath work, discipline, balance, retreat, meditation, affirmations, self-expression, nature, mantra, creating a temple, belonging, music, meaningful work, service, compassion, reflection, rituals and creativity.

All of these practices keep me in more of a joyful, balanced state, connected to my soul. Their practice enables me to do my work from a more soulful place where I make more conscious decisions, am more responsive instead of reactive and stay in touch with my natural instincts and intuition. Standing fully in my center, filled with light in my heart, my portal is open to the insights coming through.

Joy and balance isn't something you attain and then have forever. It is another way of being and it takes spiritual practice to maintain it. My little dog is my bliss guru in a way. She absolutely lives in my circle. When I'm working from my home office and I'm having a hard time, feeling stressed or overwhelmed, she shows up and says, "Lets go for a walk." I look into her dark eyes and realize she is a spirit dog. In these moments I think I don't have the time because I'm frantically trying to get something done. I'm sure you've been there: you can barely see straight but you keep working. Crazy Woman is in full force and when she shows up, my little dog reminds me I need to get out and walk. Usually by the time we get to the corner, I am already getting back into center and can feel the connection again. In her doggie energy, she is so happy running and sniffing, it reminds me that this is what I also need to do.

Having attended tons of personal growth workshops over the past 40 years, I thought I'd faced every bit of my baggage. However, nothing prepared me for the issues that arose once I decided to step in fully and grow a real business. There's not a day that goes by that I don't have to face some big issue that wants to derail me. I feel anger, shame and a million other emotions that could hijack me from where I need to be focusing. As I shared in Chapter 2, these emotions are often a wake up call that deeper insights and consciousness shifting are underway. (This part is so important I decided to dedicate Chapter 6 to this topic specifically.)

BEING WILLING

Regardless of all the issues and challenges, visionary entrepreneurs are the mavericks of the world: those people who are willing to take risks, be creative and face their own demons in the process. They are making real change on grassroots levels and sometimes in huge ways.

If you are one of those who know you can't work for someone else, that you want to make a bigger impact and you must follow your own dream, use this picture and process to help you stay on track and support your success. The world needs your contribution.

Create Your Own Success Portal

The graphic on the following page is your Visionary Entrepreneur Picture template, ready for you to fully stand in each area and notice what comes up for you.

Make this your own by filling it out. Using colored pens or markers, put words, colors or symbols in each of the three sections.

If you want a larger version of this graphic go to WiserandWilder.com/resources to download it.

I recommend printing out a few of these so you can do this process every few months and notice what's changed.

Here are a few questions to help your process. The very best way to benefit from this is to use a combination of your head, heart and hands.

Head - Listen to your brilliant ideas, wisdom and knowledge. Notice what ideas or thoughts come up.

Heart - Be aware of how you feel and what your heart is telling you. Open your heart to feel bliss, pain and your deep yearning.

Hands - Your hands are about action and habits and will remind you about taking right action. Allow your thoughts and feelings to flow through your hands and onto the page. Your hands will choose the colors.

WHO IS YOUR VISIONARY?
- ◉ What is your soul work?
- ◉ What does she want to bring to the world and why?
- ◉ What makes this so important?

WHO IS YOUR ENTREPRENEUR?

- ◉ How do you feel about your business garden?
- ◉ How are you nurturing the roots to grow stronger?
- ◉ What does your entrepreneur need to learn?

WHERE LIES YOUR PERSONAL GROWTH?

- ◉ How does it support you?
- ◉ What is it saying to you?
- ◉ What do you need to hear?

Ponder these questions. How does this help you to bring your visionary and entrepreneur together as a whole?

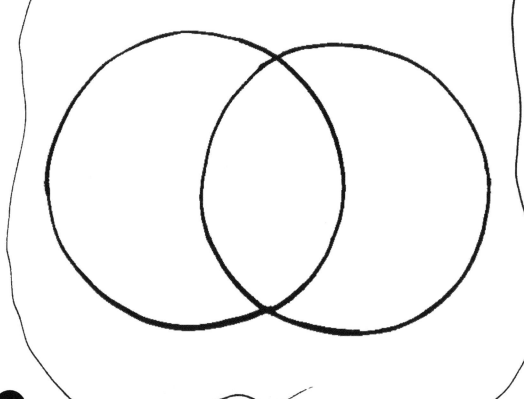

Soulful Community

"At the beginning, when I was in my early 20s, all I wanted to do was sell enough paintings to support myself. I thought that alone would be amazing. I worked hard at that, but once I got there, I realized this in fact wasn't my real work.

What I had been working at consistently for 16 years was creating and selling my work, which meant being alone in my studio. I realized that wasn't the soul-fulfilling job I wanted. It felt like I hit a wall and had to completely re-evaluate where I was at. If this wasn't my dream job, then what was?

I began talking to a lot of people I trusted and becoming part of a strong community. I wanted reflections from people. When one person mentioned teaching, I lit up. That was three years ago and since I've ended up writing a book and teaching workshops all over the world. How my career is expressed now is through helping people, which has so much more meaning for me. Working with people and being in a room with people has given more meaning to my whole life.

Now another new change is coming. Instead of flying everywhere, I am embarking on a new shift where I will invite people to come here into my space and be a part of my community. At the age I am now (40), I want to be home more with my boyfriend and my dog and friends I love. Plus, now that my job puts me in contact with people a lot, I now enjoy alone time in my studio so much more.

Many people ask me for business advice as they see me as a successful artist. My first question is, 'Do you like people?' Even though you are alone when making your art, in reality it is a people and relationship kind of job. Building strong connections and relationships is what builds businesses and if you can't do that, you will be left behind. Relationships and community are everything."

~Flora Bowley

The Power of (More than) One

Many passionate and creative ideas begin in the middle of the night. You're awoken with an inspiration that shows you a path to quitting your dead-end job and providing a way to earn money while doing what you love. So you share your ideas with friends or relatives and you get mixed responses and advice, but in the end, it must be your decision to move forward and begin the path of building a business from your soulful dream. It begins with you alone taking risks, making decisions and walking a path that is sure to be filled with ups and downs.

But building a soulful business also requires the support of the right people who not only get what you are doing but also love it. You may come to the point where you realize you need and want this, but money is scarce so you become a do-it-yourselfer.

The positive part of this approach is that it builds strength because you have to learn how to lead yourself, which usually includes learning tons of new skills, plus how to manage your own time and energy. But this can also be the most challenging part of being a solo business owner because you can end up spending hours and hours alone, mostly on the computer getting things done. Many of those things don't directly bring in cash and yet you feel it is necessary to spend hours at your screen while becoming more and more isolated. I began just this way and experienced both the pluses and the minuses.

Here is what I learned in the process.

Your business needs real live people, as Flora shared above. **Your entrepreneurial house needs to have community built right into its foundation.** This is not something to add in later. It's easy to add closets, new tiles or other remodeling to any house, but it is virtually impossible to change the foundation. The foundation is the blueprint. Community, tribe or people - whatever you call them - they are essential to any business so they need to be part of the innermost circle of your root system.

I see too many people who come to me for help after a few years of struggling to get their vision business off the ground. Many have isolated themselves doing things like creating workshop outlines, writing eBooks and interacting on Facebook, all while alone in their home office. When I suggest to them that they need to get out in front of real people, many groan because connecting with their circle wasn't built into their house foundation, so there is no room in their schedule for it. They haven't built that half of their house yet, but there's still time to add it in.

You may not realize something is missing in your business but then you start feeling anger and stress building up. These feelings can be good wake up calls telling you your business soul is trying to get your attention but you aren't listening.

What do you do when you wake up? Reach out. Community in its best form will provide love, support and collaboration - heart and soul connection. Just reading those words makes me smile, feel at peace and grounded. It is the natural antidote to the stress and overwhelm of trying to do everything yourself.

You might be thinking this is the catch because you don't have the time to go out and develop community, find your people and create your tribe. That's a big mistake because connecting with real people is the natural antidote to the stress that comes from being in front of your screen all day, as well as the depression and overwhelm that comes from going around in circles in your own brain.

It's important to know that you and your business are a part of something bigger than just you. Nothing in nature survives in isolation. Using my own garden as an example, two of us tend it regularly, providing kind hands. We have our neighborhood nursery to bring in fertile soil, the sun above provides her rays and companion plants nearby are important, as are the bees. We have neighbors who help with watering when we are away. Every so often, our gardener comes in to do weeding and heavy jobs. I post photos of my flowers on Facebook and many people comment and offer their own gardening stories, so people enjoy my garden no matter where they live.

Supporting a garden to grow requires a lot of energy. I may call it my garden but it takes a team to do it. Most people don't realize how many people are actually parts of their team because they don't count every single person who helps and supports them or their web of connections that reaches outward.

I feel like I have a whole community right here with me while writing this book. On Facebook, people offer feedback and also pop in with their own insights and wisdoms. This community, along with many others, keeps me rooted to what is intrinsically essential to me and my survival.

As visionary entrepreneurs, COMMUNITY is essential for so many reasons, but here are just a few thoughts.

- ◎ It is energizing to be a part of something bigger than just you
- ◎ The group mind with creative ideas is more expansive than just your own
- ◎ You can give to others in your circle what only you can offer
- ◎ You can tap into group wisdom that is rooted in ancient tribal circles
- ◎ You can share a group purpose that you have in common
- ◎ Opportunities for collaboration arise
- ◎ You get encouragement when you feel like quitting

How To Create your Relationship Circle

Some people are natural networkers and others are more introverted. Either way, it can feel confusing to know where to put your energy and how to develop the right kind of connections. I developed this diagram, which I call my Visionary Community Doodle, to make it easier to understand the process. Take a look at it and read about each part below. Then you can explore how to make it work for you in a way that suits your personality and strengths.

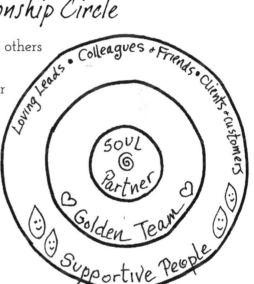

SOUL PARTNER

The center circle in this illustration represents the Soul of your business and your Soul Partner. This is the place where your Wise Woman lives. She's part of you and helps you to open your heart wisdom and listen to what's best for your soul and spirit.

Any successful entrepreneur will admit that even though their business began as their creation, it eventually has a life force of its own. Your business is meant to support you, not the other way around, and if you don't listen you will struggle much more. If you do listen, you are more likely to create something beautiful.

This concept is especially easy to understand when working with clay. Clay has its own energy too and if I try to force it to do something it doesn't want to do, it will collapse or crack. All potters know this. We learn how to be a channel, because only in this place will the lump of clay transform into something beautiful. It is its own entity.

How about Mozart's beautiful music which some people say came straight from God? Here's what Mozart said about it:

> When I am completely myself, entirely alone or during the night when I cannot sleep, it's on such occasions that my ideas flow best and most abundantly. Whence and how these ideas come I know not nor can I force them.

I see my business as a separate soul force and being as well. I didn't get this at the very beginning and just like the clay, my business ideas constantly wouldn't take shape the way I wanted them to and collapsed. I was trying to run the show but I didn't have the skill or know how, so I tried to push it in a way that was not in alignment with its energy. Just like needing to learn about how clay molecules work and interact with water, pressure and heat, I needed to learn the basic business skills. Ironically, that entire time my business was actually fine; it was just me that needed to understand it.

I now know that my Wise Woman lives in the center circle and is my soul partner, essential to my creativity and purpose. I imagine her and my business as a separate entity because this perspective helps me access information from a much more expanded place. Often what she needs is important to be heard and heeded even though it's not always what I think I want in that moment, so I need to step outside of myself to accept her wisdom.

My first business was selling pottery I created in my studio. I had a beautiful studio and was selling everything I could create, so on the surface I thought I had fulfilled my dream. But over time, like Flora, I realized I didn't enjoy the isolation of working alone. The best part of my job was going to Saturday Market each week and being part of that community. When I tuned in and listened to my soul's message, I realized I just loved the people and the connections I found there. It took many more years for my path to lead me to where I am now, but it all began with listening to that message from my inner soul partner.

One day I was trying to figure out a topic for a blog post and feeling stuck, so I went for a walk with my little dog Poppet. I was feeling frustrated and had no idea what to write about. I began walking and it was as though a silent voice spoke to me and I listened. Not only was the topic given to me, but also the outline and main points. It was brilliant and I just stopped right there on the sidewalk and said thank you. At that moment, I realized I wasn't alone and I had never been alone. She had been there all along!

I remember back when I was looking for a name for my business and was busy looking up domain names to see what was available. The name Awakening Business popped into my head and I immediately knew, 'Yes, this is it!' It felt so right and the url was available. I had to go back and make sure I had spelled it correctly because I was so surprised. I now know this was her doing. No other explanation worked for me because that should have been a high demand url.

She is the Goddess and Crone of my business who is wise and wild. She talks to me and takes me for walks, gives me words for my writing, paints and tells me to turn off the computer by 8:30 every night. For the past 10 years she has been my soul partner, so I know I am never doing this alone. I talk to her everyday and she talks to me. I still make poor decisions and get stressed, but I connect with her in the thick of the mud and she helps me to get back on track much faster than I could ever do by myself. She has an overview that I often can't see because of the clutter in my brain or my self-doubt. She probably knew exactly what soulful path my business growth would take while I was busy trying all kinds of things that weren't correctly aligned. If only I had known enough to listen!

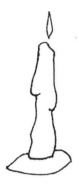 Now I know when I need to go inside and listen to my soul partner. I stop whatever I am trying to do and get myself out into nature, go for a walk or a bike ride. These are the things that help me to connect with her guidance. Also, I've developed the habit of beginning my workday by lighting a beeswax candle on my desk and then playing my favorite chant. I invite her to begin the day with me and those two acts shift my energy for the whole day. It's like having an invisible advisor and soulful assistant right there with me in my office. We don't all do things the same way and you have to find your own way to connect to your own soul partner or Wise Woman. The important thing is to listen and take heed. You might not know the next step to take, but when you listen and are open, your soulful path will appear.

YOUR GOLDEN TEAM

Take a few minutes to get in touch with your vision that passion and mission that you deeply want to keep giving birth to. You might have written about it, talked about it, begun to turn it into a business or already have a business that's set up and out in the world.

Next, imagine this vision in its biggest form, manifested just the way you imagined it would be. See it as being fully developed and helping all the thousands of people who will be receiving help as a result of your idea.

You know you could never make this happen without a supportive group of people by your side; people who also believe in your vision and want to help it and you to be successful. In order to take your dream out in a bigger way, you will need to have a team of people supporting you.

Your team is made up of those golden people who you work closely with and also offer their unique skills where they're needed. These are exceptional folks because without them, you would not be able to provide amazing service and products to your customers and clients. They all live in your circle.

Many solo business owners begin solo, hence the name. As I shared earlier, you began with your creative spark and started doing everything yourself. Watching your bank balance was one reason and the other is that you might not even have known you needed help. The third reason could be that you are having trouble standing in the footprints of your identity as someone who can manage on this level.

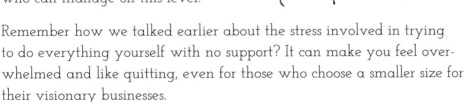

Remember how we talked earlier about the stress involved in trying to do everything yourself with no support? It can make you feel over-whelmed and like quitting, even for those who choose a smaller size for their visionary businesses.

If you don't think you have a team yet, here's a quick activity to help you get started:

1. Take a moment and think about all the people you have hired in the past year to help you.

2. Write their names on a piece of paper and tape it to your wall.

3. Put this list in the bottom right corner of your office (the space for supportive people in the Feng Shui bagua).

4. Leave extra space on that paper to add more names.

The most important piece to know here is that all these people are part of your team circle, whether you hire them for only a few hours a week or for special projects. Just this small act will remind you that you actually have a team.

Another way to help you shift into growing your team even more is to make a mind map of every type of role you would want filled and how that person would support you and your dream. These become job descriptions in a way. Once you do this, people will show up to fill those roles like magic. Eventually you can add names. Doing this short activity will help you to expand your mindset around what a team would look like.

This process can be used for a new product you're launching as well. I have done a version of this for my book creation because I know I will need many people to help me take it from an idea to a published work out in the world. Some of those pieces I wasn't even sure about, but once I wrote it all out, I was able to fill in little bits at a time to make a rich colorful mosaic work of art.

No matter what you choose to do, be sure to listen to that wise soulful part of yourself and then you will find the right people who get who you are, what your values are and the spirit of your business.

Remember the saying, "It takes a village to raise a child." It also takes a village to build your vision.

SUPPORTIVE PEOPLE

Supportive people are those in your tribe who love you and what you stand for. They are like the fans at the Olympics who are cheering on the skaters or gymnasts. Those hundreds of people give you strength and make you remember that you are doing your work for so many more people than just yourself. Thirty years ago, if you were a rock star or other idol, those were the people who would fill your mailbox with hand written letters telling you how much you meant to their lives. Yes, there used to be fan clubs that many people joined so they could live vicariously through someone else's dream.

Supportive people can be loving leads (people who follow you on social media or email and love what you do), colleagues who you have built heart-felt connections with, or clients who you have intimately worked with in some way.

Loving Leads

Social media has changed the way we look at this part of the circle. Suddenly, almost overnight, it's possible to develop deep connections with people you have never met in person and may never meet face-to-face.

If you perceive yourself as not being a 'people person' and you've stayed away from social media because you don't enjoy it, it feels like a waste of time or you just don't see the point, you have an attitude that isn't going to work in our world today where social media is essential. Here's one example of how it can work for you.

Your Facebook friends page alone can connect you with thousands of supportive people very fast. Take Flora who we met at the beginning of this chapter: She posts regularly, showing her newest paintings, photos of her workshops, her dog and her at the beach, her new house, her mom, etc., and she always has at least 50 people commenting and hundreds of people liking each post.

People love her and want to be part of her supportive people circle. They connect deeply in their comments, sending her love when her mother was dying, celebrating her new art, and supporting her in many more ways because that connection and community is so important to them too. They want to be in her circle. This is one big reason she has been able to grow her business so seamlessly. It is not by accident or luck.

Yes, it takes time to write a post and then go back and acknowledge people who have commented, but it is time so well spent. It certainly takes less time than going to a local networking group, if you count the time it takes to get dressed up and drive there. You can do all that networking while in your jammies sitting by the fire.

I've seen people try to hire someone to do Facebook posts for them but that doesn't work as well. This is one thing you have to do yourself because it needs to be YOU people are connecting with. One of my friends tried this and I felt it right away so I stopped commenting or liking her posts. I asked her about it later and she admitted that as an experiment, she had hired someone for a while. I wasn't the only one who could feel it.

Facebook groups are another great tool. If you want to connect with people who have the same interests as you do, joining groups is one of the best ways because there is no limit to the number of people who can join. You can also start your own and invite people. What a good place to share your vision, get feedback, create trust, build community and grow your reputation! You can join my FB group here: facebook.com/groups/WiserandWilder/.

As a business owner, you need to be a part of multiple communities because, depending on where you are in your business, some fade away while others step in. Supportive people can include colleagues, mastermind groups or Facebook friends and family, all people who love you and what you are doing.

Take a moment to think about all the people and communities you are a part of. Which ones really feed your soul and why does this happen? Community is about Communing + Unity. Do your groups carry this energy? Are they really your tribe? Can you be totally yourself and be appreciated for your contribution?

In order to grow and nurture your supportive community, you need to really step into a place of leadership in yourself. It means standing in confidence and knowing that part of what you are offering is being a model for others. Are you ready to be that person?

Collaborative Colleagues

Part of the Woman's Way is embracing collaboration instead of competition. Competition can turn you into Envy Woman and bring out your worst parts where you compare yourself to others who appear to be doing better than you. Or you might adopt a scarcity mindset that says there aren't enough clients to go around. If you follow the trail, this kind of reaction takes you right back to your self-worth issues.

The opposite of competition is embracing your colleagues as wonderful people who might overlap a bit with what you offer, but in the end, it offers people a choice. Stepping into an expansive and open mindset like this is so much healthier for you. **Your colleagues become people you love; you love what they are doing and their energy and you want to be part of their tribe as well.**

These are also the people you can collaborate with for mutual benefit. For example, my podcast, Business the Wise Woman Way, is filled with interviews with my colleagues. Some of them I barely knew until we did the interview and now I feel like we have a much deeper connection. I celebrate their successes, re-share their posts on Facebook and stay in touch with them. Sometimes we even see each other at live events. I know that when I decide to do another joint venture, I have a whole list of people to invite to join with me.

Your business will only grow so far without these kinds of partners.

Luckily, as women, we are good at creating relationships, so forming these kinds of business connections is easy. Once you make this decision, you will immediately see your business expanding to a higher level.

Clients and Customers

Your clients and customers are often the most supportive people in your world. They have hired you, paid you their sacred money and many will rave about you, refer others to you, write testimonials about you and re-share your posts on Facebook.

There are things you can do to make this easy for them. The most obvious is often missed: showing appreciation. Appreciation is so easy and has such deep reaching effects. One of my clients, Elizabeth and Jeff Spitzer, created what they named an Appreciation Board. Liz said her idea grew from a place of feeling unappreciated by her blended family. Their board encourages families to take the time to show appreciation for each other. To learn more, go to https://theappreciationboard.com/

Some people give their clients Starbucks cards or other small gifts, but for me, the best kind of appreciation is expressed on social media because it is read by hundreds of people.

Not only are my clients parts of my support group, but I am part of their teams as well, so we live in each others' circles. When my clients complete their work with me, I offer them numerous ways to stay in touch and I can also stay connected to them. It just requires awareness and an intention to get out of the dysfunctional DIY mindset and look for and create opportunities to nurture strong relationships that will go on for many years.

As your business grows, you as the visionary entrepreneur will grow with it. You step into more empowerment and eventually you will have an elder business, one that is all about mentoring at its core.

The Visionary Community Doodle showed you the three main areas you need to expand in order to connect with your soul and your people. Are you ready to be that person who has all of these pieces alive and vibrant in your business and in your life? Or does this still feel like a huge mountain to climb for you? In the next chapter, we will be looking at fears, self-doubt and other beliefs about yourself that might be holding you back from building a strong community. Take heart, you will get there!

Your Community Circle

Now that we have explored all three rings of the circle from page 69, it's time for you to create your own. In my workshops, I have had people create the circles on the beach in the sand and notice how it feels to stand in each area. You can do the same when using paper and colored pens. Possibly use a different color for each of the three circles.

Draw your own Community Circle on a large sheet of paper free-hand and let go of needing it to be perfect.

Using the principles of mind mapping, put your consciousness into each area. Beginning with the center circle, go into a mindful place and ask these questions:

- Who is your Soul Partner?
- How do you get in touch with her?
- What does she bring to you and your business?

Then go into the next circle and ask:

- Who is your team?
- What roles still need to be filled?
- How do they or will they make a difference?

Finally, step into the outermost circle and ask:

- Who is currently part of your support circle?
- Who would you like to include?
- What value do/will they bring?

Write down everything that comes to you, writing in the margins as well if you like.

Breaking Free

"In my last year of college I committed to doing a senior project. I knew that if I did it successfully, it would allow me to build on my perfect grade point average and graduate summa cum laude.

I had already proven myself with essays; now it was time to show 'em what I could really do. I aced a handful of creative writing classes so of course I felt that much closer to my dream. Eager for the challenge, I brought my writing samples to the head of the creative writing department. She read them over, asked me a few questions and then agreed to mentor me through my project. We had an entire semester to work together, nearly five months to mold my rough drafts into genius.

One month away from the deadline and eager to see how we'd tie up the fruits of my labor, I met with her one last time. In a voice that felt ten degrees colder than usual, she asked me to sit down.

'I'm sorry. This work isn't cutting it Téa and I don't think we can salvage anything,' she said.

"What do you mean?" I replied, feeling the blood leaving my head.

She then informed me that I was going to have to scrap everything I'd written and start over. Offering no suggestions on how to move forward, she added, "This is what needs to happen. Do it or your project is over."

I don't remember leaving her office or getting home or even crying. I only remember the deafening quiet of my home later that night and me tucked into a fetal position with my best friend at my side alternating between her soothing whispers and my raging tirades.

The next day I realized I wasn't ready to give up so I girded my wounded loins and made the rounds of my creative writing professors. Unfortunately, I was discouraged by everyone with words like, "Kid she's a freakn' department head. If she says it won't work, I'm not gonna fight her on it."

The only option they had for me was to use one of my better essays and work with the head of the literature department instead. Utterly deflated, and yet holding tight to my dreams of creative brilliance, I decided to throw in the towel and opt out of the entire process. My Bachelor's degree now reads merely 'with honors.' No summa cum laude for me. It's a first world problem to be sure, and I got over it. Eventually.

But first I endured a pummeling of rejection letters from graduate creative writing programs and months of unemployment peppered by the odd temp job. I felt like I was living at the bottom of a deep dark well and there was no way out.

Ultimately, I let that experience kill my dream. Not once since I left college have I written a poem or a short story. Whatever muse I once had got on a bus that summer and left for greener pastures.

Now I write blog posts and articles and marketing copy, but every time I try to give life to a story? Nada. It's not a conscious choice, either; it feels more like someone surgically removed the piece of my brain that could make stories up. There was just nothing there, so I told myself that those are things fiction writers care about, not business writers.

However, one nagging internal voice wouldn't go away. It seemed to be asking me if I was ready to infuse my workshops, coaching and mentoring with a more prominent focus on creativity and voice. Soon I got a big YES! and now I am finding my way back."

~Téa Silvestre Godfrey

This chapter is all about liberating whatever might be holding you back from your magnificence and how to trust your deep wisdom so you can do your soul work in the world.

Like Téa, most visionary entrepreneurs are a unique species. We are Wild Women motivated by something deeply primal calling us to rely on our raw feminine instinct when making our place in the world. Colors, smells, inner knowing and the song of our womb provide the map forward toward our life purpose, our gift of service and our reason for being.

Some part of your very being knows exactly what you are meant to do. If you trusted this, you would find your way up out of your well, through the rocks and brambles or whatever has you trapped. Gradually, you would grow in strength and depth and begin to shine.

Your decisions would all come from those roots.

However, many women like Téa end up getting sidetracked because they are told that who they are is just not good enough. Others are told that they aren't smart enough or able enough. It's worse when this happens when you are at your ripest, bursting forth with so much light and just putting your toes in the water. At those times you are so vulnerable, like Téa was when she presented her most sacred creative genius only to have it coldly rejected by someone older, supposedly wiser and with greater authority. She was told that who she was at her core wasn't acceptable. When this happens, we unconsciously sever that piece of our very being and then regroup, attempting to continue to have a good life without that soulful part.

Sometimes, rejection isn't so blatant. For some of you, it's about what you weren't told, which can be confusing because it doesn't feel like real neglect. You were fed, loved and provided for; you just weren't seen as the bright spirit you were because no one saw the real you. Children's services would never come out to your house and give your parents a warning for not recognizing that they had a child who was destined for greatness.

Out of the thousands of women I have talked to, I have not met a single one that didn't have a story about a wound that was so painful they chose to move on without it being resolved. They simply continued on in their lives with that unresolved piece left buried out in the Siberia of their psyche.

When you decided to begin your business venture, your wounded part came along with you and affected many of your decisions from that unconscious place. No matter how bad it was, there could still be many outcomes, just like in a novel. The one you have been living is your version of what happened and, yet, there is another version you could choose that might shift everything.

Trying to Fit In

Many of us grew up in homes where no one saw the true brilliance inside of us. This was my story and the longer I wasn't seen, the more I adopted the habit of just wanting to fit in and not stand out. Insecurity became my middle name and for years I had no idea of who I was. Any creativity I had as a little girl was squelched out of me by the 1950s public school system, where not only was I not seen, but my round little spirit needed to become square to fit into their box.

I spent many years uncaging my wild spirit on the beaches of New Zealand with my women's community and then ended up coming back to America to be closer to my only child. Upon return, I decided to do my business for real for the first time, which triggered all my past fears of not being seen or acknowledged. Here are some of the fears I felt:

- Not being smart enough to make it in business
- Looking like a fool
- Doing something that wouldn't work
- Speaking out and being criticized
- Being wrong
- Colleagues thinking I was flaky
- Being seen and also of not being seen
- Being too old

I fully engaged myself in learning all the practical wisdom pieces to get my business going and yet I felt like a shadow version of myself. I cried, had panic attacks and feared my soul was gone. In fact, I had left her, my Wild Woman, in New Zealand, the first place that ever felt like home to that part of me. I needed to call her back to me if I was ever going to make my business work.

Finding Your Own Wisdom

In Chapter 4, I talked about the importance of personal growth to help you blend your visionary and your entrepreneur. I explained how the more unfinished past issues you have, the more confused you will be when trying to access your own voice, your own wisdom and your own genius. We looked at how these emotional triggers can cause you to lose days if not months of energy.

Your Wise and Wild Woman is a mixture of your soul wisdom and practical wisdom. You need both parts to be fully alive and successful. Like many women, I had split my practical wisdom from my soul wisdom. I followed practical logic and developed my business offering what I thought would sell, rather than what my soul needed to be doing in order to thrive. I did this from fear and not trusting who I was.

One of my colleagues positioned herself as a marketing coach because, as she says, "I didn't think anyone would be interested in what I really do (strategy, finance and operations). I thought nobody would pay for it. Even though marketing is part of what I do, it actually isn't big enough for me."

Like me, she also shied away from showing herself fully and attempted to build a business from something that felt safe but wasn't her real passion. For both of us, our inner doubts made us fear that we didn't have the ability or brains to get where we wanted to go. In response, many starting out in business decide not to try because they don't want to be seen as a fraud. Or they erroneously assume that no one would pay them for that, so instead, they base their business on something they think is sellable. But then they don't do that well, because their souls just weren't into it. Can you relate?

If you are someone who has taken the mistaken path, the only path that seemed open to you at the time, and have ended up in a place that is not truly your place, it could be because of fears, confusion, self-doubt or many other "unseen" reasons. You might wake-up one day and ask yourself, "How did I get here? Why did this happen?"

Surprisingly, it's not really that important to know the reasons why. And recognizing how it happened is important only so you can go back and rescue that part of yourself who lost her way. What's more important is to begin to see yourself in your truth, who you are and what you are meant to be doing. It is never too late.

I know many women who go out and get more and more training, more certifications and more papers to frame and hang on their walls, thinking this will make them more qualified. However, at the end of each course, they end up right back with their Wounded Healer who calls them to really look in the mirror with no make-up, just their naked selves with all their weird blemishes.

Your challenge is to say hello to your lost self, welcome her back from the underworld and encourage her to grow her roots into Mother Earth and stay with you, so your Wise and Wild Woman can be a complete whole and your true wisdom can emerge.

Kathleen Hanagan, a dear friend and colleague, shares:

> As a healer over many lifetimes as well as in this life where I was the oldest of seven children, I have always had to know and in fact be the teacher in order to survive. But essentially I always felt alone because I could not trust letting anyone see my fear and even hid it from myself.
>
> When I say I needed to know in order to survive, I mean just that. I put myself aside and instead honed the gift of seeing what

is true for others in order to survive in an emotionally charged world with a fierce and fiercely loving father.

Then, at 57, I responded to a call to embark on a journey that included a descent into the underbelly of the online marketing and coaching world. I cut myself off from my roots as shaman and medicine woman, as well as from my feminine self. I jumped on a fast train that was so focused on money that I soon became bereft.

What I was re-experiencing was the deep aloneness that many Wounded Healers carry when they have lost their sense of soul purpose. So I decided to stop listening to anyone who claimed to know the solution or have the magic key and instead chose to surrender and be open to guidance in a new way. I am not really sure I had much choice in the matter, as I had truly lost my way. My inner strength helped me to move forward.

Today, at 63, I am back on track. I am more open to love than ever and enjoy vibrant health because I truly unpacked the bags of fear that had been zapping my energy. Within my wound was my way to true wealth. Now my teaching comes from deep knowing.

Your Wounded Healer

I think all women entrepreneurs of every age face this Wounded Healer part of themselves over and over. Kathleen is just one who deeply felt the split, the severing of her two parts.

The Wounded Healer often appears as self-doubt and can stop you dead in your tracks. Oddly, there really isn't anything wrong with self-doubt, but the Wounded Healer takes it to an extreme, where you find yourself in a deep hole, like Persephone going into the underworld, and your self-judgment keeps making the hole deeper and the wound bigger.

From that broken place, you make broken decisions that are based on your soul's separation and all the fears and distortions that go with it. Both wisdom parts are needed in order to create not just a business but also a way to make a big difference in people's lives and the world as a whole.

If you attempt to build a successful business only from practical wisdom, it won't work. As Kathleen shared, you can learn all about marketing, finances and business planning and you'll have some success, but eventually you will feel like quitting because your soul is somewhere else. Your soulful wisdom is the sap in your business tree and without it, your tree won't grow, thrive and put out an abundance of fruit.

Melting Away Self-doubt

Most women plummet when self-doubt arrives. It can feel like running straight into a wall and smashing against concrete. It actually hurts and you feel like a portal is closed to you. You sense there is a doorway there, but you feel as if it's not yours and you would have to be somebody you're not in order to pass through it. If you let self-doubt become your truth, it begins to sap your energy and you begin to question your own wisdom.

I write a lot about self-doubt, not because I am obsessed with it, but because I'm actually an expert in this area from experiencing so many years of it being my alter ego. It wasn't until one day in my mid-50s that I looked in the mirror and realized I was finally okay being who I was. I felt a calmness and rootedness to the earth that I had never felt before.

I tell my clients that self-doubt might always be there, especially when you are stretching and trying new things. It's one of the first things all of my small business clients share, regardless of how long they have been in business. Even for successful veterans, self-doubt can feel like a parasite at times, glomming onto your body and short-circuiting your wiring. My advice is to treat self-doubt like the wicked Witch of the West. Notice her, confront her and then turn on the hose and watch her melt away.

I'm not saying that this applies only to women, even though some theorists propose that men tend to be over-confident while women are less confident. Regardless, women aren't competing with men in their business, or with other women, because there is enough room and enough clients out there for anyone to be successful.

You aren't even competing with yourself, but when you compare yourself to the self who you want to be, and then judge yourself for not being that person, you might as well be.

Self-doubt, shame and the fear of being seen are all tenacious. Those parts can grow bigger and bigger and take over, keeping your real Wounded Healer so small that you forget she is there waiting to be welcomed back. I am reminded of a plant with sharp thorns called gorse that grows prolifically all over New Zealand. Some people see it as having no value at all, but in fact, Mother Earth knows better. Bees love gorse and gorse can even rejuvenate soil after it's been disturbed by concrete or other unfriendly substances. That's some power! Just like gorse, your fears have huge power that can be transformative in helping you to wake up and restore the soil of your soul.

Rituals for Empowerment

Now that I am in my Wise Woman years, I still have self-doubt moments, but not as often and they don't last long. In fact, I find that each trip I take into the underworld of self-doubt awakens me. When I resurface, I usually have gained valuable new awareness similar to what happens in an empowerment ritual. I've done hundreds (maybe thousands) of these kinds of rituals with myself and with other women.

We stood in a circle on the beach and each women was instructed to find a piece of driftwood that symbolized her true voice, what she wanted to be seen for and her true genius. After a meditation and visualization, we all stood with our driftwood pieces, which became voice wands, holding the magic of each woman's true brilliance. One at a time each woman spoke with a pure strong voice, stating her truth, and then each stick was placed in the center on the sand until we had a sculpture of visionary gifts. Everyone could see how each woman's contribution was part of a beautiful whole creation.

I also used to do sand tray therapy when I was a counselor. I loved this tool because it allowed people to create and witness their own world with symbols. I still use the bones of this process to help women get out of their box and get moving in their businesses. See the activity at the end of this chapter for more details.

Are you ready to join this circle of women who are creating visionary businesses based on their real genius? Like most visionary women, you may need to rescue your soul by making that journey into the underworld, your shadow place, before you can enter fully into your circle. This includes facing your fears head on as this is where your power lies.

The ritual process for this is different for each person, but without your whole soul and spirit, you will end up trying to run a business without this big piece of yourself.

First you need to go deep inside and find that part of yourself that has split off and ask what you need to do to bring her back. It's that simple.

Next is the harder part: following through with your message, which can mean making big changes in your life. From my experience, these changes are almost always positive shifts, but they could require letting go of attachments that are no longer serving you. For my journey, I was told I needed to find my community where I could be wholly myself and be seen for my true soulful contributions.

In order to keep your Wild Woman vibrant and spirited, you need to be vigilant about keeping the vital balance between your soulful and practical parts. For most of us, this requires taking time for ourselves to replenish so we can do our work in the world without getting exhausted, overwhelmed or stressed, as these will also cause us to abandon our souls.

To begin, I suggest my clients find a spot where they can ask and listen for what they need. The important thing is to call back your soul. For most women, this means being in a place with no distractions, where you can connect with yourself and allow your real inner truth to emerge. You might ask questions out loud or you might just quietly reflect on your situation and be open to hearing answers. What needs to change or shift? What do I need to let go of or what do I need more of? Ideally, I like to be out in nature. However, even in the busy city I can always find a place to light a candle and tune in.

The important thing is to stay in balance so you can access both your soul wisdom and your practical wisdom while running your business. If you sit in this state of BEINGness, you will thrive and be able to do your true life work.

Here's a summary of how to create your own listening ritual:

1. Find your spot where you can listen and ask for what you need.
2. Go deep inside and find the part of you that has split off.
3. Ask her what she needs in order to come back.
4. Listen to the message.
5. Follow-through.
6. Find supportive women to be with.
7. Embrace both your soulful wisdom and practical wisdom.

Creating Your Wisdom World

THE PERFECT BLEND OF SOUL WISDOM AND PRACTICAL WISDOM

In this activity, you will produce an amazing power piece to place in your office or studio. As you call forth the best qualities of both your soul and practical wisdom with symbols, they will activate in your own psyche during the process of creation and then hold these energies in place for you. The benefits will continue to grow as you add things to it over time.

PART ONE: GATHER YOUR SUPPLIES

1. Fill a large tray or cake pan with sand.

2. Find a handful of small flat stones.

3. Get two objects of your choosing, one to represent your soul wisdom and the other to represent your practical wisdom. These can be objects from nature, collectibles, toys or something that speaks to you. Tune in and trust your intuition to find the two objects that best symbolize what you want. They might be human figures, animals or anything. Just one restriction: These objects need to be small to fit in your tray.

4. Assemble a few waterproof marking pens of various colors.

PART TWO: BEGIN YOUR RITUAL

1. To begin, I suggest you find a spot where you can ask and listen to what you need.

2. You are ready to create your wisdom world. Light a candle.

3. State your intention of creating a world where your soul wisdom and practical wisdom will work together to support your success in the highest way possible. Ask to be given what you want and need.

4. With your hands, move the sand around until you have created the environment that feels right. It might be flat or have a hill, a river, spirals or whatever feels right to you.

5. Place your two objects in the sand terrain wherever you feel they should live. You can move them around until it feels right and it feels like they are living in harmony and power together.

6. Using your marking pens, write words on the stones before adding them to your wisdom world. Your words will come from your wisdom.

7. You are also welcome at this point to add any other objects you feel will support the union of these two energies and will help support your intention.

Place your wisdom world in a spot in your workspace that feels right. If you aren't sure, you can place it in the far left corner, which is your Feng Shui prosperity corner. You can add more word stones or other objects anytime you feel a need.

For more information about how sand trays work, go to WiserandWilder.com/resources

CHAPTER SEVEN

Money Wisdom

"My father was an entrepreneur so, seeking approval and emulating him, I got my MBA and became a business banker in a large Boston bank. It was a male dominated profession and I was a young attractive chick. I'm sure this helped me land the job but I had to excel twice as much to be taken seriously.

All my clients were business owners and I lived vicariously through them, but I didn't really get their struggle because by that time I was earning up to multiple six-figures. I was a real yuppie who owned property, travelled and bought expensive stuff.

When I vetoed some unethical lending practices I lost my job suddenly without any warning. As a compulsive spender, I had high credit card debt and absolutely no savings. I lost two homes and fell into the poverty experience. It was a shock to realize I wasn't going to be making six figures the next week.

I was lured to North Carolina for what appeared to be a lucrative business opportunity, which promptly fell through. I discovered that my credentials meant nothing there. I started my energy healing, spiritual counseling practice and was barely getting by. I was deeply wounded and didn't realize the extent of it until I hit rock bottom. Then I was evicted, went bankrupt and my ego crashed.

Ultimately, I ended up going back to what I am good at when my energy healing clients kept asking me if I could help them with their finances. That's when I realized I had thrown the baby out with the bath water. I am in fact a highly strategic thinker and I love business, and I was missing both in the healing work.

I started to look at my numbers and my own spending. I realized I was spending 60 percent of my money from my healing practice on healing myself because I was such a mess. Gradually I began to come out of it.

Working on my own financial situation woke me up as I began to track the details of money in and out and the internal drivers behind money choices. As I turned things around in my own financial life, I wondered if what I was doing for myself would work with others. I started working with two acquaintances and saw real transformation from my approach.

I'm 64 now and am realizing it is more exhausting to hold back a calling for expansion and more energizing to just trust that the next step will be there. My message to older women is that soulful work can enliven you. At our age, women have a valuable inner presence that is deeper and more compelling than physical attractiveness. We as healers, teachers, and world changers have to get over the whole money thing that keeps us limited. I want women to take responsibility, do their inner work, tend to their money and numbers and get on with it, because we all need resources to do the fabulous work we are capable of doing.

It has nothing to do with the economy or money controllers and all that stuff. There is a lot of unholy stuff going on in the world but that's not what is keeping money from us; we are holding it from ourselves.

I've always resisted the Crone, as she seems stern, a bit like my kick-ass banker persona. I would now rather be the soft magical grand-mother type, but I am embracing that stern part too because she has the power. I can be soft and supportive but I will also kick your butt to do what needs to be done to ground the resources you need.

I am fed up with the scarcity marketing going on that people get sucked into. They claim they will help you make six or seven fig-ures, but really I believe it needs to begin with you taking responsi-bility for your own evolution on a much deeper and comprehensive level than just revenues."

~Aine Dee

Money Illusions

This chapter is all about money mindset and growing in money empow-erment. Money issues can be like cobwebs that grow into corners where you don't see them until you do a deep housecleaning. In this chapter, we'll be looking at those dark corners that you might be ignoring but are still there, attached to other things in your life with their energy-zapping tendrils.

To me, dealing with your money issues entails facing your truth and calling in your wisdom. **The first step, which needs to happen way before anything else, is to know where you are and why you make certain decisions.** Then you can learn how to BE someone who is confident and worthy, and therefore can have an abundant business.

I decided to begin this chapter with Aine's story because she has blown a hole in the illusion that if you just **had** a job with a paycheck, everything would be much easier. In some ways, it might be easier because you could just count on X amount of dollars each month and wouldn't have to do all the work of **marketing** and business planning. However, as Aine has just shown us, unless you do the inner **work of** being financially responsible, you could **end** up just like she did, booted out of your job with no savings and no back-up plan.

There are so many highly skilled, creative, visionary women who can no longer emotionally cope with a job. I hear this echoed by **hundreds** of women who feel their wild spirit **would be** smothered and stifled if they were to **again start** working for someone else, so that door is **closed** to them.

Women need to have their body, soul **and spirit** nourished in order to thrive and do **their work in** the world. Making the decision to launch **a** business is a big deal and many of the fears that arise are based in the root chakra, that place of feeling safe, supported and taken care of. Believe me, I know. This was the hardest chapter in this book for me to write because I am still fully working on my own money wounds and I certainly am not yet a money expert.

Your Money Story

Navigating the world of money has been my greatest challenge right from the beginning. I fluctuated between being a money avoider and a spontaneous spender. Somehow I would spend everything I earned and then avoid looking at my bank statements out of fear that I would see a zero and wouldn't know what to do. I had a love-hate relationship with credit cards. I hated them but still ended up using them to buy plane tickets, transferring my balance from one zero interest card to another.

As I neared my 50th birthday, I decided I needed to change this pattern and learn how money works, how to earn it, how to get rid of debt and how to be responsible. It was time.

At first, it was hard for me to get help because I was embarrassed to tell anyone the truth about how irresponsible I had been. I remember how I handled money 25 years ago when I taught Reiki workshops in New Zealand. Even though I had large groups, I asked everyone to pay in cash, collecting it all in a wicker basket. My secret real reason for the cash was so that I wouldn't have to deposit it and pay taxes. I still feel embarrassed writing this today, but I have to tell the truth. At one point I had over $10,000 in cash hidden in my room under my mattress. No, I am not kidding. I just didn't see myself as a grown-up around money. I was acting like a kid who was getting paid pennies and keeping them in a piggy bank.

I was still living a polarity of 'us and them' back then. I was someone who wasn't smart with money so I wasn't a real business owner. I was a healer and an artist and I didn't believe I could earn big bucks consistently or know how to manage it. This was my secret. The 'them' were people in suits with briefcases who had accounting degrees or were just born with a money gene that I didn't have. You might notice that I didn't include anything about my personal choices in that description.

I didn't recognize all this until I began the descent into my own underworld where I had to speak the truth like an addict at an AA meeting. I had so many wonderful qualities: I was highly skilled in my work as a counselor, facilitator and educator; I had two masters' degrees; and I had helped thousands of women to heal and transform. However, when it came down to it, my self-worth couldn't accept any of that until I also got the money part working.

I attended a variety of workshops about healing money wounds and yet the real work didn't begin until I had to put what I learned into action and develop new habits.

Over the past 20 years, I have transformed a lot of the pieces that kept me stuck and I no longer struggle financially. This is a big one because I remember when I would wake up with panic attacks, worried that I would be living under a bridge someday. The panic attacks disappeared when I began to trust the money flow, which happened as I started to believe more in my self-worth. I am doing a lot better, putting money into savings and tax accounts every month, but I am still making changes and learning because transformation and self-growth really never end for any of us.

Worry
Debt Failure
Lack
Fear

I know some of you who are reading this have your own shameful money secrets and I highly suggest you share them with someone. Tell your own story. It is transformative and the first step to waking up. One way is to use Luna Jaffe's book, *Wild Money*, along with the workbook that goes with it which will help your story to easily appear.

By the way, before we go on, my book is not a how to book, so I'm not going to include tactical money management stuff for you to do. If you do want help with that, get Luna's book.

Self Worth and Money

I realize now that being savvy with money isn't about meeting financial goals and thinking that once I hit X number of dollars per year, I will be healed. As Aine just showed us, it has nothing to do with how much money you are earning. It has to do with your self-worth.

Do you feel you, as a human being, are worthy of having a good life that includes flourishing, being safe and being taken care of? In our world, money is the ability to provide this for yourself. If you don't think you are good enough or worthy enough, it won't matter how much money you earn, you won't be able to keep it. This was my story and the story I have heard from hundreds of women I have spoken to in the past 15 years.

As part of my research for this book, I had conversations with over 100 women entrepreneurs and asked each one about their money issues. Almost every one shared that they want to thrive financially so they can do their work and have the resources they need to touch more people, while being able to live their lives without money stress.

Everyone wants financial security like this and can taste and feel that kind of prosperity, and yet so many highly brilliant and gifted visionaries are still struggling to just survive. There is a huge canyon-size gulf between what people want and yearn for and what they actually have right now, even after many years in business.

Here is what I heard from people I've talked to. Which ones do you relate to?

- By accident I fell into offering something people needed and was earning $8,000-$10,000 per month. It was amazing but I had no idea what my expenses were and how much I owed on invoices, so I ended up going bankrupt.

- I work long hours to market my services and have done tons of social media and local networking, but I have been avoiding the money part because of fear or discomfort. I am embarrassed to admit I don't really have any records.

- I am very attracted to shiny objects and have spent $20,000 on big name programs that promised me a six or seven figure income. I believed them and so deeply wanted it, but instead I ended up with even bigger money wounds and no closer to wealth. I am angry for being so stupid and actually feel like a failure as a result and don't trust myself to make good decisions.

- After years of study, I know I am a brilliant practitioner, but I'm a horrible money manager and have no idea what I actually earn and where it goes. Money goes in and goes out. I have no budget. I'm not proud of this.

- My husband has a high paying job that supports me and I feel embarrassed because I see others struggling and I'm not, but really I'm a fraud because if he wasn't there, I'd be out on the street.

- I have a bookkeeper who does my accounts every month so everything is tracked in QuickBooks (QB), but I don't really know how I'm doing because I don't know how to read my own profit and loss statements or what to look for. I barely know how to open QB myself.

In my generation, women weren't really taught about financials or expected to be money managers, so many of us never even thought about money, other than having just enough to pay the bills. Even Aine, who was a financial whiz, didn't get it on a personal level until she crashed.

However, this is not a generational issue. My clients are age 30 and up and most of them have big money issues that keep them struggling in their businesses.

As I mentioned above, I put off writing this chapter because in some ways I felt unqualified in that I'm still dealing with my own money issues. However, in other ways, this actually makes me the perfect person to write this chapter because I've been dealing with money blocks my whole adult life and have had to look in the mirror and deep into my own soul to discover where I got off track at an early age. I explored how my decision to not focus on making money and my tendency to spend money I didn't really have, got me into deep trouble over and over. Eventually, I decided to change my story. To do this, I had to change my habits.

I have had to force myself to change my mindset that said money management is boring and hard. I also had to rewire my brain so that when income comes in now, I don't see it as money to immediately spend. The funny thing about money is that when you keep it around it actually multiplies and grows and can then be reinvested in yourself, which is perfect once you feel worthy.

On the other side of the coin are the hoarder/savers who can become so constricted that they don't take necessary risks and choose to stay small and safe. Where's the balance here?

When it comes to money, I've learned that it matters not whether you are a spender, a saver or an avoider. How you operate and make money decisions are always directly related to your self worth and confidence. Regardless of your primary money type, you can always be responsible and have a positive relationship with money.

Read through the stories in the next section and notice which ones you relate to. They each illustrate a mental block that can keep you stuck. Understanding them will help you get clear about what's keeping you from realizing your earning potential. Once you face your blocks, you can make the best changes.

Money Traps

Here are two examples of self-talk that can sound logical when inside your own head.

If I charge the price I feel it should be, no one will be able to afford it.

How many times have I heard clients projecting their own scarcity mindsets onto their potential clients? Not really a surprise when you consider people often tend to market to clients who are similar to them. If you are earning $30,000 a year in your new business, you might feel uncomfortable with clients who are earning three times that amount. Unconsciously, you think, "Why would they want me?"

In fact, they won't if you have low self worth and lack confidence. Again, the first place to begin is with your own personal growth.

I shouldn't charge as much as someone who's been doing it longer.

It is true that someone who has been in business for a long time and developed a reputation will be able to charge a higher amount just based on that. However, most people who make this statement are basing this on their lack of confidence and thinking they aren't as experienced and therefore not good enough. The truth is you might be just as good as the person who has a stronger reputation. In fact, many of those people who are charging a higher price have way less training, but they have a lot more confidence and a strong marketing plan that they actually implemented.

If people really deeply need help with their problem, they want to hire someone who is very confident about helping them. It's rarely about the price when it comes down to making a decision. People want the person who they feel will be offering them the best service and help.

The irony about pricing services is that it needs to be based partly on what you need to receive in order to support your business and yourself, and partly on the benefits your clients want and need to receive. There is a give and take. People who pay for particular help need to know it's money well spent. If you aren't confident, it won't matter what you charge because people won't pay it. Your clients can have tons of doubts about themselves but you need to be empowered and clear in the value you are offering.

However, I never encourage anyone to charge more than they are comfortable with, but comfortable often has to do with your own confidence, so looking inward is still so important.

How much do your decisions still come from a scarcity and fear mindset? Confidence about the ability to manage and understand the world of money is something many women feel shaky about. They just can't seem to feel worthy of earning money and they are afraid of investing. Even very professional, highly skilled women often hide from or avoid these money issues.

Money Shadows

There are money beliefs that live deep in your unconscious that can affect decisions and ways of being. The goal is to become more aware and bring them into the light.

Greed and lack of heart

Some people are driven primarily by money. Is it any coincidence that many of them lack compassion? When that happens, the shadow side of greed can creep in.

Debby, a 32-year-old, contacted me for business help to learn how to more effectively work with her employees. She had started her office cleaning business right out of college and built it from nothing to a multiple six-figure business in five years. She was proud of this.

In our first session she ranted about how her employees were bleeding her dry because they didn't work efficiently. Constantly focused on her bottom line, she showed very little appreciation for the people on her team and the hard work they did. As a result, they weren't happy and eventually they would all quit.

Debby wasn't able to see her contribution to this pattern. She came from a very poor family. Her dad was an alcoholic and her mom was a victim. As she grew up, she decided that would never happen to her, so she studied business with her whole focus on not turning out like her mother. She assumed this was a really good choice as evidenced by the fact that she was making money, saving for retirement and breaking her family's cycle.

However, she got migraine headaches regularly and in spite of taking heavy-duty drugs, she would wear sunglasses all the time as the light hurt her eyes. At the beginning of our work, she wasn't able to see that her fears of not having enough and the unfinished issues from her childhood, were making her sick. That's the problem with the shadow trickster. You can bar the door and it will find another way to sneak in.

When she began working with me, she thought the issue was with her employees and didn't have a clue that the problem was actually with her. After months of working with her, she gradually opened like a glacier cracking. The pivotal moment was when I suggested she thank her people for all their help and hard work and give them gifts of appreciation. She screamed out that she had worked hard starting at the age of eight and no one had ever thanked her, so why should she. She was that starved little girl again, now in tears.

Somehow she agreed to do what I suggested and that was the beginning of helping her heal her past and developing a whole new way of running her business. On the financial level, her business had the best year ever, even though she also raised the salaries of all of her employees. Her clients began to love her employees since they were happier and thus doing a better job, so her referrals increased and she was able to hire more people. Her migraines began to disappear as her heart began to open.

Givers and Rescuers

Some women have deep needs to be loved at all cost. See if you relate to any of this description.

It is your natural way to want to give and give more. You are so worried about looking greedy that you disappear rather than ask for money. Even when you do ask for money you are uncomfortable, so you immediately want to lower the price. This is a much more common role for women to fall into than greed, actually. It is way easier to offer more and more for free than to confidently ask for payment.

I had one client say to me that she would rather be poor than look like she was greedy. What a black and white way of thinking! Of course there is a third choice, which is to be an empowered, confidant woman with high self worth. But instead, many of these women keep on struggling in their businesses, which keeps them feeling deprived and lacking prosperity. In their heads, they believe in the ideal of prosperity but they don't practice it. It's as though they want to be given money without having to ask for it.

This is shadow side of you living too much on the visionary side and not enough on the entrepreneur side. It's that feeling that you need to just do your good work and make it not about money at all, either because of a spiritual conflict or because you just want to do what you do and not be bothered with marketing, planning or anything you don't enjoy. But your business gets out of balance when you never deal with your money issues (personal growth part) so ultimately you cannot succeed.

For artists, it can **mean giving away your paintings**, while **for coaches it can mean** giving away too **many free sessions or** not knowing how to charge. For spiritual practitioners, it can **be waiting** for the universe to **provide.**

My therapy background often tempts me to analyze people and wonder what causes them to **make certain** choices, but I try **to steer myself back** to the present. By **getting to know** them and their businesses in the present, I **eventually** start to see **the part of** them that is either **missing** or asleep.

Often I see a half-built house. One side is **beautiful** while the other is **only half built,** or maybe even just **a hole in** the ground. The beautiful half is my client's **amazing** work in the world that is so important, soulfully **real and** needed. It is her **soul wisdom** that her Wise Woman holds in her heart.

The unbuilt half of her house often represents her business mindset or the practical wisdom that is necessary for every entrepreneur. Money management lives in this unfinished half. Without that part, the other half just keeps taking over. That's where you put your energy.

For many years I was like a slow moving turtle with only half a shell. In order to build the other half, I had to face my money wounds, grow in confidence and see myself as someone who is smart and able to be a leader of my business. It has been my life work in a way.

The 'I only want to do what I enjoy' Syndrome

Have you ever complained about having to do stuff you don't enjoy?

If you do this only occasionally, it's okay. But if this is your regular mantra, pay attention. This could be why there is a hole in the ground instead of the other half of your house.

Amy started a business offering a specialized form of bodywork that included shamanic healing plus deep work that would change one's limiting patterns at the core. She had an extensive amount of training and wanted to move on from doing basic massages and begin to attract people who wanted this new work that she enjoyed doing.

We talked about her needing to be more visible and to develop a marketing plan that might include making some videos to post on her website and social media, doing local talks and joining networking groups to get herself in front of people and build her reputation. I suggested that she make choices based on her comfort level first and not do all of this at once.

We also discussed setting up an auto-responder email process so she could begin to be in conversations with people who opted in to learn more. As we talked about these ideas, she began to wilt. She claimed that doing all that kind of technical stuff made her go out of balance and feel stressed, which she feared wouldn't be good for her. Even local groups seemed too stressful. At the same time, she was flat broke and in tears off and on about how she needed more money, so she couldn't hire anyone to help her. We talked about how she could make these activities fun and she still disappeared.

She had a large, large hole where the other side of her house needed to be, but she would rather keep struggling than put out the energy to build her completed house. She could not get the concept of needing to shift her mindset so she could identify as an entrepreneur as well as a healer. The healer in her was the only one making the decisions. She wasn't integrating her soul wisdom with practical wisdom. She hadn't learned to trust her inner Wise Woman to help her stay in balance and learn how to work in a way that was less stressful and more enjoyable. The opportunities to learn those habits are part of the house blueprint, but you have to be willing to step in fully and make a decision first.

Many women have their own version of Amy's story and make decisions from what they enjoy doing and don't enjoy doing, rather than what needs to be done in order to increase cash flow. In Amy's case, her self worth was based on her ability as a healer and not on being a business owner. She needed to expand her identity and her self worth to include being a successful leader of her business and someone who could attract a whole new group of people to work with her based on her visibility in the community where she lived. Once I put it that way, she started to get it and her whole stature began to change as she started to feel more solid and successful.

Family money values

You came from a family who imprinted their values on you around money. It is a rare person who can avoid this modeling. As children, we learn from our parents and this includes all the stuff we listen to.

I have a close friend who has had low paying jobs his whole life and always refers to "wealthy people," as "them." He thinks of himself as one of those people who never has much money, never will, and just accepts that as who he is. As it turns out he had learning disabilities as a child and was told by his mother and step-father that he wasn't very smart and that he was basically worthless. He adapted that message and lives by it now.

He could shift and change, but it would mean digging into the core of his being to find who he really is and then make choices from that place. It would be a healing on deep levels. Not everyone wants to go there.

I also talked to someone recently whose parents were both in real estate. Her mom was an agent and her dad was an investor and they worked together, so their conversations around the dinner table were all about real estate deals. Tanya and her siblings were included in the conversations and asked their opinions at a very young age. She remembers the excitement of these discussions.

Is it any surprise that Tanya grew up and had her first house when she was 20 and now owns a string of rental properties? She is an artist and is one of those rare artists who has her work in galleries across the country. She also owns three Etsy sites, has produced a variety of products with her designs and does well financially. Her early imprinting carried over from real estate to her art business. I would consider her to be someone who has a high amount of confidence and money savvy.

It is the rare person who manages to create a different financial worth than what they grew up with, without doing the inner work. You could be telling yourself you are not going to be like your mother, and yet, unconsciously you end up doing the same thing.

What was the dinner conversation like at your home? What was discussed and what did you hear? I imagine there are some things you want to bring forward and other things you would rather leave behind.

Money and Motivation

If you are motivated by either passion or wanting to make positive change in the world, money often isn't in the picture to start. This not being motivated by money is not a bad thing; in fact, it can be a plus because people who are totally money driven can lack the balance between head, heart and hands necessary to making it through those tough periods which can happen in any business. Look at Aine who we met at the beginning of this chapter who had a high salary, but had nothing in savings when she lost her job.

Passion and sense of purpose are perfect motivators to get you moving on your idea. The excitement of really stepping in, making a difference or doing the thing you love will keep you going when you feel like quitting, which will happen when you hit a wall somewhere down the road. The yearning for money won't help you to get past the struggles that happen to everyone who starts a business, but passion will, at least initially.

But when that sense of promise at the beginning begins to fade and your phone isn't ringing and your bank account is starting to get depleted, then what? It's discouraging to have put so much energy out to get your business launched and then fall into the pits when you don't have money coming in and not enough clients. It can make you feel like a failure and worthless. You begin to question if this can really be your soul's work if it's so hard!

Money is a huge barometer of success in the entrepreneurial world, especially with all the hype around getting six and seven figure incomes. It's painful to compare yourself with those people who seem to offer no better services and products, but are earning real money when you are barely in survival. Again, you need to let go of comparing and turn right around and look at yourself, your money issues and what you need to do to change.

You might want to dive into the personal growth section of the Visionary Entrepreneur Picture in Chapter four again, to help you locate and face those blocks that are keeping you stuck. Willingness to step into the money part of the entrepreneur circle will also enable you to create your own personal Money Map, which spells out how much money you want to earn and where it will come from. Go to WiserandWilder.com/resources, to download my easy Money Map Template.

I do believe that visionary, intuitive women can change the world in positive ways. The potential is there. It's like ripe fruit just ready to be picked. But you have to expand your capacity so you can grow your business larger, touch more people, make a bigger impact and be a stronger leader of your business.

To do all this means facing your money issues and developing empowerment in that area.

Are you willing?

Your Money House

This process is focused on giving you more insight about your money issues and how they might be affecting your ability to create prosperity from your vision.

To begin, go into a place of mindfulness and feel into each of the areas listed below. Just notice what comes up for you.

- Self Worth
- Money Management
- Saving
- Cash Flow
- Giving and Receiving

- Confidence
- Spending
- Avoiding
- Greed
- Family Money Values

Take notes and observe what memories or feelings arise. From that place draw a picture of your Money House below.

Once you have drawn your house, go to
WiserandWilder.com/resources,
for questions that will help you interpret your drawing.

Seasons and Cycles

I met my husband at Cornell where we both graduated with bachelors in electrical engineering. Still in my 20s, I thought I could be just like men career-wise, so I began my career with feelings of promise. I worked hard and felt happy with my success for a while, but when we moved from California to Oregon, I found that many of my fellow workers were men with stay-at-home wives. This bothered me but I became determined to be the exception.

When I got pregnant with my first child, I felt conflicted because I believed I could be just like the male engineers and continue to climb the corporate ladder, but I also had internal programming about what a mom was supposed to be. I soon found there weren't enough hours in the day to do both jobs to the level I expected of myself, so I requested to work part-time. But then I became exhausted because it felt like I had two part-time jobs, both of which required full-time energy. I soon realized that the idea of men and women being equal career-wise was, at least for me, a lie and this made me very angry. I felt betrayed, but I struggled on to keep my part-time work, even though I felt like a failure both as a mom and a professional.

Because I was so out of balance and trying to do it all, I started experiencing actual physical pain. My heart literally felt broken. Finally, in defeat, I quit my job, which made me feel happy at first because I was able to stay home all day with my son. But then, while my husband continued to work from 7 in the morning until 7 at night, I became isolated, lonely and bored. I felt desperate to do something productive and started using anyone one who would talk to me as a therapist.

One day while reading a programming book for fun, I began to toy with the idea of building websites for others. I fantasized about receiving the praise and feelings of success I craved and had been missing since I quit. As my goals became clearer, I hired a business coach to help me make a business plan that would compliment my lifestyle and values. For each year, we projected the number of hours my children would be in school and scaled my financial expectations for my business accordingly.

This all began when my boys were 3 and 6 years old. They are now 9 and 12 and I have since grown my business from a one-woman show to a team. We are having an impact on so many peoples' lives through our work that I now dare to say I am building a company.

I am still doing the job I was trained to do but not in a corporate setting. Instead, I work in a way that blends with my whole life. Having created one life out of my two jobs, I now define success differently. I suspect when my kids leave home, I might bring some of my 20s energy back, but in a different form. I'll be able to take what I've invented that's really my own and grow it bigger if and when I want to.

~Jocelyn Mozak

Moon Cycles

Women's adult lives are all influenced by a silver thread of connection to moon cycles, sometimes called the Triple Goddess, which includes the life stages of Maiden, Mother and Crone. No matter what nationality, color or income level, we all have this same invisible relationship with the moon and our sisters.

Our cycle begins with our first blood and ends when we are leaving this life. During the years in between, we choose our life path, but everyone experiences the influence of these monthly and developmental cycles because all women are born with a womb, which is our energy center. The blood becomes a river we travel from puberty through menopause and then our blood transforms into greater insight during the Wise Woman years.

Right now, you might be wondering what this has to do with Wise Woman entrepreneurism, but it does! I've been working intimately with women of all ages for the past 40 years and I haven't met a single woman who was not highly affected by pregnancy, child-raising, period pain, cyclic energy fluctuations, menopause the list goes on.

As Jocelyn shared in her story, because we are women, these personal issues can't be separated from our businesses. In her case, her business was birthed as a response to having children. She shaped her business to allow her to experience her life all as one, rather than the separated bits that made her sick at the end of her corporate job. I've found that the only reason Jocelyn or any woman tries to separate out parts of them-selves is in an attempt to fit inside a box that is not made up of their values.

Certainly, to function in the world we do have to keep things compartmentalized somewhat. However, at the same time, it is so important to acknowledge the truth about who we are as women, which includes being holistic beings where every part influences the others. This is what Jocelyn meant by her business allowing her to have one complete life now, rather than trying to separate out parts of her life in order to fit into a world that doesn't see it this way.

I still remember my shock when I found out at age 11 that I was going to bleed every month for the next 40 years. I was freaked out. I wondered what else I hadn't been told about being a female. During my teen years, we all called it 'getting the curse.' I had one friend who was in so much pain every month she had to miss school. I wondered why she had this reaction to normal monthly ritual and how she would manage in a job later in life.

Until fairly recently, the work world has been male dominated. Molded by a male culture, the higher levels of corporate businesses are still almost always controlled by men and operate from that culture. This isn't balanced and hasn't worked for many women who have had to mold themselves into a way of being that is not inherently part of their make-up, which is more holistic and includes all the parts of their lives, not just the identity they have in their cubicle.

In recent years, many women-owned business have emerged as well as progressive companies that have expanded their values to be more aligned with how women naturally are. This includes acknowledging emotions and intuition as assets, creating space for women to use breast pumps or breast-feed their babies during work time and allowing them to work from home when necessary.

One of my favorite comic strips is Stone Soup by Jan Eliot. One strip showed a woman with a computer live stream of her child's day care so she could watch him while she was at work. Women can't cut their lives into pieces and forget one part while they are doing another. We are just not made that way.

As women, we have to balance our professional lives with our natural cycles and developmental changes as they arise. These changes show up differently for each woman, but they always show up, so to pretend that you can fix them or make them go away is paramount to living out of sync with who you are.

We can get childcare when a baby appears, but this doesn't take care of our emotions or sleepless nights. Likewise, we can take herbs and use acupuncture for hot flashes, but they are not just superficial symptoms to get rid of. Something very deep is happening inside and it can interrupt your sleep or make your mind foggy all day.

Coping with these changes while working is no small challenge, regardless of whether you are working for someone else or running your own business. The latter has one big advantage, however: you can prepare for these cycles very consciously in the way you set up your business. Those of you younger women reading this, it's my hope that you will get this.

Now that I have picked up the staff of the Crone, I can look back and see that if I had understood what I am going to tell you next, it would have made a huge difference in many of my struggles throughout my entrepreneurial life. I pushed myself when I should have rested, I rested when I should have been proactive and I could have made better choices and had more empowered outcomes.

I say to my women clients, put your health, wellness, spirit and family first. This is not what we are told by the male model of business. I don't think the stress and "put work first" focus is good for most men either, but that is their book to write. Just because you put your kids first doesn't mean you aren't powerfully committed to your business success. It just means that the way you operate will look different.

The Triple Goddess

The triad of Maiden, Mother and Crone can be used as a metaphor for the different stages of entrepreneurship, and understanding which stage you are in personally will affect your business.

My hope is that this section will support you to flow with the river rather than fighting the rapids. **Using the power of the moon, our guardian in the night sky, will help you navigate your business ship so you are able to stay on course while you plant your business garden and grow multiple money stream crops.** The Almanac was correct: You can plant seeds anytime, but when you plant root crops with the new dark moon, they do much better!

The triple moon represents the Maiden, Mother and Crone as the waxing, full and waning moon. These labels are symbols but what's important is the meaning behind them because that's where the gems are found.

The Maiden

The Maiden of the crescent new moon represents the promise of new beginnings, youth, excitement and a carefree erotic aura. It's the time of life to freely explore and take risks while following dreams.

On a personal level, this is the stage from first bleeding to most of the way through your 20s. You see your whole life in front of you, years and years, so it's time to try things and experiment. There is a sense of spaciousness that if something doesn't work, you can try something else. Maidens are the dreamers and that fresh new energy exudes from their veins. If you are in the maiden stage of life, you might feel the urge to take more risks, follow your bliss and use your youth to enlist help from people who may not offer it once you are older. Maidens can also be a bit shy as the moon is still forming and they might not trust the world yet, but they still want to step right in and grab opportunities.

On a business level, a Maiden is young and new. Her business is newly conceived with that naiveté of newly stepping into the world, when there is excitement and a sense of promise at the beginning. A brand new business has this innocence and passion. During this stage, there is likely little or no cash flow yet because systems are still being put into place and you may not have a marketing plan to speak of. You are trying things out and finding the right message and correct niche. The Maiden business often lacks consistency and conviction while trying to get more clarity and develop business habits. Often, there is a focus on how to get clients, as this will not only bring in money but also give you confidence that you are on the right track.

Positive energies of this stage include: excitement, feelings of promise, and creativity while dancing the dance of lustful flirting with that beauty of shyness. People will be attracted to helping you and want to give advice and support because they are attracted to helping young women who are just waking up to their potential.

Often, there's little feeling of struggle or failure in this stage at first, as you are in the process of finding your way. But soon, challenges do arise as your new yummy energy can only last so long. The mistake most young women make is not getting help soon enough, thinking they can figure it out themselves.

As I shared in Chapter 4 about the Success Portal, being a visionary you might tend to focus on what you are good at and where your passion is and ignore the business building parts. This will come back and bite you in the next stage, so the task here is to recognize that your moon is only a crescent and is still growing. You need to grow with it in order to use its energy to the fullest.

In this stage, the springtime energy nourishes new seedlings that want to grow large, like the moon. Watering and feeding the roots of your new business tree is going to help it grow stronger, put out fruit and eventually be a strong grandma tree, but at this stage it needs to have the hot sap running through its veins while it digs its strong roots deep into the soil.

The Mother

The Mother of the full moon represents ripeness, fertility, fulfillment, stability and power. Whether or not you have given birth to children, you are in the Mother stage, which is about taking responsibility for yourself and others. Its energy calls you to listen to what you need for your own survival and how to stand fully in the place where you are meant to be.

Women work hard at this time of life, whether or not they have children. From an astrological perspective, this stage begins with the Saturn Return (age 28-30) and has to do with stepping into being a grown-up (Saturn is about personal responsibility). Very often, this stage begins with a personal crisis not unlike the crisis Jocelyn told us about at the beginning of this chapter. She was 27 when she got pregnant the first time and went to part-time. Then, at age 30 when her second son was born, she quit her job.

This stage ends in the early to mid 50s, depending on when menopause happens. There are really two parts to this stage. During the earlier, more outward years, women step into being an adult and working hard at whatever they are birthing, whether that be raising children, career building or owning their first home. It's a time to give it all you've got while remaining reliable to yourself, your family and others who are important to you.

When menopause begins toward the end of this stage, it takes you more inward. It can feel like a shock as your hormones change and you undergo an inner metamorphosis. You may experience a loss of energy along with grief for what was, as this stage often coincides with children leaving the nest or older parents dying or needing your help.

The Mother stage of your business is when the hard work of building your business is in full bloom. You have a sustained cash flow but want it to be bigger, so you begin looking at how to grow other income streams. If you are a solo-entrepreneur, you might be looking at how to leverage instead of doing it all yourself, burning the candle at both ends and not seeing enough result for all your effort. You are growing in visibility and therefore attracting more solid leads as well. The Mother stage is characterized by the hard work of business development and learning how and where to spend your time and energy for the best possible outcomes.

Your full moon business wants to shine, be the star, be distinctive and attract attention. Standing more fully in your distinctiveness requires digging in on the deeper levels to discover your mission and who you are. That's why one of the biggest challenges of this stage is knowing where to put your energy. Women can be such hard workers that they spend too many hours working on something that may go nowhere. Overwhelm is one of the biggest issues in this stage. Mothers try to juggle a million different things at once and have a tendency to be do-it-yourselfers and not get help.

Other challenges involve wanting to stay safe and making decisions from self-doubt or fears, versus really being out there. For example, you might know that you need to schedule a local event, but you are held back by your lack of confidence. These conflicts can be especially painful because this stage's full moon isn't happy when it's hidden behind a cloud.

The Crone

The Crone represents the waning moon and she is all about pulling inward and sharing wisdom from her heightened awareness. The wise woman teaches from her life experience, greater intuition and visions during this time of reaping and harvesting. Crones feel called to speak out and can have their greatest impacts during these years. The wisdom of this stage is often accompanied by an attitude of confidence and self-acceptance.

On a personal level, at this stage a woman's body changes as her hormones shift again. It begins when menopause is complete and there has been no bleeding for 14 moons. Some women experience grief and low energy in their 50s, but then a new energy source emerges that includes heightened intuition and inner sight. Women at this stage know who they are and what they want for the next part of their life. Rather than building like Mothers, or dreaming like Maidens, the Crone stage is more about BEINGness.

As women move into their 60s and onward, physical challenges can begin to creep in which can make you feel like your body is falling apart. However, the Wise Woman knows that she must flow with it and focus on the inner planes, which are so much stronger than ever before. The hard work no longer calls to her; instead, her path is about mindfulness and stepping into what she has to give back. This is a time to enjoy a rich community of spiritual support and love. Women are reaping the successes of the past years at this time and asking themselves what are they called to do in this next stage of life.

On a business level, the Crone business is stable and has systems in place to expand, leverage and grow in whatever way it wants to go. The waning moon calls you to think and build deep instead of wide, harvesting what has worked and expanding from that place. This can involve strong joint-venture partners and others who will support your business strength. A higher cash flow comes from the careful building of systems and income streams, and a strong team is in place to work with you. You have stepped into being a leader of your business and you now have the freedom and spaciousness to be the visionary you want to be and create your legacy. This could include writing a book or creating a podcast about anything that you know about deeply and can teach others. The key is to involve other people and their resources.

Ironically, one of the biggest challenges of this stage is its many opportunities. Making the best choices becomes more important than ever because those choices will transform your focus and take you down new paths.

If you began as a solo business owner, there might be a tendency to still think in terms of DIY, yet thinking about doing everything yourself now makes you feel tired. The waning moon is telling you to expand past yourself and bring in a strong team to support you so you can do your real work.

The Mixing of Moons

There is a lot to be learned from looking at yourself and your business from these perspectives. What happens if you are personally at one stage and your business is at another? For instance, beginning a Maiden business when you are a Maiden is very different than when you are a Crone starting a Maiden business.

In the past decade, over half of new women-owned businesses have been started by women aged 55 to 65, so both the issues affecting Crone and Maiden businesses are crucial to consider while building the business. On a personal level, the owner is experiencing waning moon energy while the business in its New Moon stage. Likewise, some Maidens or early Mothers have Crone businesses; they have worked hard and done well planting deep roots so they are already reaping the rewards.

Can you see how their Maiden energy might influence their choices and decisions with their Crone business? Perhaps they are taking more risks or worrying less about money, or maybe they have more energy to stay up late and brainstorm. If they are smart, they will be thinking longer term while looking at business growth, how to expand or how to invest.

On a personal level, as the owner of your business I hope you can see how knowing whether you are a Maiden, Mother or Crone will help you use the assets that come with each stage in ways that will enhance your business. As women, we all carry the collective unconscious memory of these stages of female life. Even at my personal Crone stage, there are times I call in Maiden energy when I want to feel free to dream, take risks and dance with the winds. Likewise, I call in the energies of the Mother when I need to work hard on a particular project I am growing and building.

The important thing is to really acknowledge that as a woman, you are affected by your fertility cycles and it is so much easier for both you and your business if you go with the flow.

Triple Moon Activity

For this fun activity, get out some colored pencils and play some vision-ary music. You will be coloring both of these mandalas, creating one to represent your personal stage and the other your business stage.

To begin, grab a piece of paper and make two columns, one for personal and one for business. Then re-read each section (Maiden, Mother, Crone) in this chapter. As you read, use colored pencils to jot down words that resonate with you. *Note:* The words you choose to write in the personal column might be very different than the business words.

Now ask yourself these questions and use your answers to expand your notes. Notice whether you answer them differently for each mandala.

- **Energy:** Do a barometer reading of your energy level in general. How do you feel in relation to where you were 10, 20 or more years ago? How would you define your energy today? Do you give out a lot to others or is this a time to be more inward?

- **Wisdom:** How much do you trust your inner wisdom? Do you seem to have wisdom beyond your years? Maybe you feel wise in certain areas and blind in others.

- **Resources:** What kind of support do you have? Who is really there for you? Who can you count on? Are you lacking in resources or are you abounding?

- **Experience:** How would you define your life and business experience? Does it come from long years or from study?

Now, use your notes to fill in your mandalas. Remember: These images need to be all about how you feel in this moment, so encourage yourself to feel free.

When you are finished, compare the two circles. They will help you understand the advantages and challenges you have based on where you are personally and where your business is.

Once you complete this process, notice what new awarenesses you have gained. Ask yourself questions about how you can run your business in a way that will be more aligned with who you are.

Personal

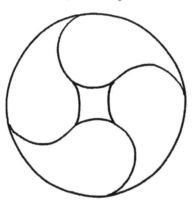

Business

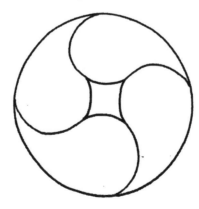

Download a full size template of these mandalas on WiserandWilder.com/resources

Crone Medicine

For the longest time, I was part of the corporate world. I was right in the fire and felt I had made it, but I was really just doing the bosses' bidding and it was non-stop. Then one day I knew I had had enough. It felt like a deep sigh. I just knew I couldn't do it anymore. I was almost 60 and now I am almost 70.

There were advantages to the job which I took for granted, like prestige. I had a high profile, but then when I quit, my phone stopped ringing. I realized people only wanted me because of my job, not because of who I am. It pushed me into a time of my life I wasn't prepared for, so I struggled a bit. I didn't know anything about business. All I knew was I wanted to keep learning and do my life work.

Today, it enrages me that the media projects imagery for people in my age group that shows retirement centers with elders sitting around a pool sipping champagne. It is very idyllic looking but also unreal. This is actually a time to be fully engaged with life.

I have now written eight books and recently my first historical novel. The whole world of 'indy' publishing with all its technology was totally new to me and I have had to learn it. I am also teaching others now and want to help women who under-value their gifts. I am doing what I am meant to do now even if the world isn't set up to include people in my stage of life.

~Lindsey Dawson

This chapter really almost wrote itself, as it's my voice, my rant and that of millions of women like Lindsey who have followed the river of blood until it waned and stopped. What happens to women at this time of life was a mystery to me and yet now that I have arrived here, I get it and see that the possibilities to fully engage with our strengths and life purpose are profound. My life story reflects my own unique evolution. When I was younger, I decided I would be different from the usual stereotype of an old person when I reached my 60s. I would still be working at a career I loved and making a difference. I wouldn't be 'old'! I thought old was a state of mind and I refused to see myself there. In my youthfulness, I had a way of not seeing what I didn't want to become.

I remember hearing Barbara Marx Hubbard speak about 30 years ago. She must have been about 55 then. She said, "I have more energy now then I have ever had, at a time when the world tells me I am supposed to be slowing down." I smiled and wanted to be just like her.

I never thought I would retire at age 65 because I never have had a job to retire from and I assumed I would always be doing something meaningful. However, when that time came in my life, just like Lindsey, I was unprepared for suddenly being invisible and not fitting into the media's stereotype of what this stage of life was supposed to be all about.

Recently, I looked up the word 'crone' in a thesaurus and was shocked by the list of words I saw on the page: witch, shrew, bitch, beast, old woman, battle-axe, biddy, fury, nag, hagfish, offensive old bag, slut, sorceress the list goes on and none of them are pretty.

To me, a Crone was a female elder who held great wisdom and had inner sight. She could create magic and commune with nature spirits. I also saw her as someone who had an esteemed status in the world. How could my definition contrast so sharply with what I saw in the thesaurus? The words I found there seemed designed to disempower women when they are actually in the height of their power. How and when did the Crone definition get changed, I wondered? I was confused. Then, when I turned 57 and had experienced one year of no longer bleeding, my women's group offered to do a Croning ceremony with me.

I had mixed feelings because I didn't feel ready to be that age, and of course those negative descriptions were still in my mind. Not being fertile anymore affects way more than one's ability to have children. I was attached to my young, sexy body and I also questioned my ability to offer anything else that would be important in this lifetime. I imagined the 45-year-olds replacing me. In a way, I bought in to the very same attitudes I was criticizing. I had no idea who I was anymore.

But then my sisters created a deep ceremony that involved looking backward and forward and it was powerful. Ironically, I was the first one in my group to reach Crone status, which I now know was a clue that my future path would include being a leader.

In the ceremony, I was gifted a beautiful staff decorated with beads donated by each woman, and I remember thinking that I would need to grow into it. I didn't realize it then but I was an emerging Crone and this powerful staff would help me clear the rocks and weeds off the path as I walked into my true power.

Ironically, a decade later I found myself in another women's circle with a group called The Women of the 14th Moon. There I had the opportunity to step up, have another ceremony and receive a new staff. I had no idea why I needed to do this twice and why I would need a new staff but I jumped up and said YES! I felt the energy so strongly that I had to do it. The Goddess of the 14th Moon chose a staff for me and once I held it I knew that this was my real elder staff, where the other was my emerging staff. Taller and so much more powerful, this staff gave me a place to stand individually as well as a place to stand for all women who will really step into their true life work when they reach this elder stage of life.

A Native American elder participant looked at both of my staffs and said the first one was more masculine and the second more feminine. This made sense to me as it's the strong female energy that is guiding me now. **She is a shape-changer goddess, wrinkly hag and woman of wisdom, all in one.** In fact, she is the one who is writing this book. Without her I would have nothing to say. She works her magic on the inner planes and I don't always know what I am going to write next until I check in with her.

Likewise, there have been those hard days where I felt like I had nothing to say and what I was writing was all crap. Then she reminds me that there is power in walking into that shadow place where I feel barren and invisible. Each time she has been right. Those horrible days have always been followed by brilliance channeled from my invisible supporters.

I bought *Power of the Crone* by Clarissa Pincola Estes and began listening to the recordings. She reminded me that the word Crone comes from the word crown and refers to a halo that shines brightly and brings clarity. Clarrisa says, "Corona (meaning crown with a luminous halo) is the one who sees far, looks into spaces between worlds and has the ability to see through the hearts and souls of others."

I still don't know what happened in history to extinguish this true definition of Crone and to instead substitute only negative words like those listed above, but for eons we have had no word for a strong elder gifted woman in our Western culture.

In fact, when the river of blood begins to turn into a trickle and then finally stops, you don't suddenly become barren and haggard. A metamorphosis takes place and you gently move into a time of great inner sight and strong presence. This is the time when your real life work can happen because you see clearly and can mentor others.

The years just proceeding, when you are in your 50s, can be a bit hard as you go through a transition time. Many women in their early 50s begin to notice a drop in energy and confusion between wanting to step up and do their true life work, and at the same time, just wanting to take it easier, to be out in nature or rest. Some women have more clarity about their soul purpose when they are 30 or 40, at a time when their energy is popping. Others who haven't had that drive and clear vision, struggle when they hit 50 and think they missed their chance and begin comparing themselves to others.

I wish someone had told me that my energy would come back ten-fold after menopause, as this stage of life is all about opening a conduit to POWER. It's about preparing your body and spirit to do its real work in your 60s and beyond. Not only did that power emerge for me, but also insight and heightened intuition that allow me to see things much more clearly than I did when I was younger.

Find your Inner Crone

Yes, I have had to do my inner work as always and yet, the rewards are there.

Why is the Crone Stage So Important?

You might wonder why defining the Crone stage is so important. Why not just be it and let go of describing it? I have to do this! Not just for myself, but for all women of all ages. I've been standing up and supporting women to be authentic, empowered and successful for over 40 years. This has been my mission and now I am carrying it on into my Crone years.

Many men can relate to this too, but for us women especially, we were expected to look and be beautiful and sexy! Smart and successful were good, but it helped to be hot as well and I knew this from age 14. I looked at 60-year-old women and saw them as 'old,' which wasn't a positive adjective. They were lovely grandmas and making a difference in that way, but were they also elder speakers, doing something meaningful in the world? No, those models didn't exist for me. Zero. You might be one of those people who is reading this and immediately think of one or two women who were the exception for you. Yes, and I celebrate them with you, but let's also acknowledge that it certainly hasn't been easy for them.

Regardless of what number age you are, you will eventually become 60, 70, and 80, so it's about beginning right now, wherever you are, to accept your authentic self and stand tall in it. The more you can do your inner work now, the easier it will be to expand on it when you enter your Crone or Wise Woman years. Plus, if you begin embracing that deep wisdom now, you will be able to incorporate it into whatever stage you are in.

Develop the habit of not hiding your truth and instead look for what it is that makes you truly unique. What do you offer that only you can give?

Like Lindsey, many women begin a new business during their Wise Woman years or their present business moves to a new level at this time. Their business is based on their real purpose, passion and life contribution, which includes all the wisdom from the past years along with the amazing insight and power that only comes later.

Beauty and Wisdom

Our society still enshrines youth and the beauty that comes with it in regards to women. In America especially, there is a bias towards youth in general, thinking that everyone will be less innovative or cutting-edge as they age.

Even though how you look and the energy of those hormones during the Maiden stage is magnetic, I wouldn't trade it for the inner gifts I have now. Even when I had that youthful beauty, I was always intuitive, but now it's super magnified. As a result, I can help people by drawing from a much deeper wisdom.

I have had to wake-up to that gift and own it. It's no longer about just being sexy, which can be hard since we are trained to use that kind of energy in our marketing. However, being real and standing in that rooted power spot actually includes sexual energy transformed.

If you've been a visionary, you will now be a visionary magnified. Inner beauty becomes the new benchmark and this requires no make-up to cover up wrinkles! It's all about what's on the inside. I love supporting all women to really go for it and use their power for fueling their entrepreneurial success.

At age 68, I still have outer beauty and younger women also have wisdom. There is an overlap, but no 70-year-old has that sexy, hot look of a 30-year-old. And no 30-year-old has the wisdom and power of a woman who has tapped into that power source at age 70.

I challenge you to look at your own attitudes about yourself and your power and wisdom. How much of it is affected by your age?

You can begin this process of embracing yourself now. Whatever age you are, allow your wisdom to come through in whatever form it takes.

It's about stepping fully into life and not hiding!

I just read an article about Frieda Lefeber, who had her first gallery art show at age 100. She went to college in Fine Arts when she was 85 and still drives and goes to the gym everyday. Suddenly, at age 68, I feel very young. Certainly our standard definitions of age and comparisons of old and young are no longer working.

The Crone Polarity

Many people only see the Crone's shadow side of ugly old hag. Even women find the word crone repulsive for this reason. The truth is, there are many mornings that I look in the mirror and that old hag winks back at me. I see the wrinkles, especially when I wear my reading glasses, and have to accept the whole enchilada. So the Crone is both the dried up, withered woman and the gifted seer woman, esteemed goddess, Earth Mother and Wise Woman. **Are you able to accept all parts of yourself?**

Funny thing is that men can also be seen as older and uglier, but they are still regarded as having sage wisdom. Because women's value has traditionally been based on being young and beautiful, it can be hard to put yourself out into the world once those hormones disappear.

In order to still be doing your life work at age 70 or 80, you need to begin to look in the mirror and see both the light and the shadow. Even that cantankerous old woman has a certain power. She's the one who says, 'I don't give a shit anymore. I'll say what I want and wear what I want to wear. If people don't like it, it's their problem.' Every woman I know past menopause feels and speaks this way.

Part of the real Crone energy is knowing you aren't going to fit into any conventional definition of what a women your age should act like. I

started to wear my hair in braids recently. I love braids and yet I wondered if this was professional enough. I decided I didn't care. That was my Wild Crone Woman speaking. She doesn't care so much what people think anymore. In fact, if she stirs people up, all the better.

When I shared a photo of myself in braids on Facebook, a friend informed me that many spiritual Native American women wear braids as they are thought to connect outward like areoles or haloes. If I'd only known, I would have done it sooner! So, put your hair in braids and join me.

My Shadow Crone showed up in my body a decade or so ago when my knees started giving out. Eventually, I was in so much pain that I couldn't stand on a stage to speak. I could have asked for a stool and brought a cane, but I didn't want to look disabled. Yes, not looking disabled became more important than speaking. Crazy, I know! Now that I have had both knees replaced with shiny new chrome ones, that issue has disappeared on the outside, but I find myself not wanting to tell anyone because if they don't know, they won't think of me as old and falling apart.

Can you hear this? How hard it is to be self-accepting? So now I am writing this for the world to hear because my need to share and support all women to be empowered in who they are is more important than my fear of being judged or pigeon-holed. It wasn't easy to get here, but I could not have written this book until I arrived in this place of accepting both sides of my Crone.

Another hurdle appeared for me over the last few years as my hearing started failing. In some ways, this was even harder because hearing aids are connected to old age. Children wear glasses so they are not seen as age related, but hearing aids are definitely for old people. All I could do was to really look at HER, a deaf old hag, really accept her and then go get the hearing aids.

I only need them when I am with someone who whispers or mumbles, in large groups of people or in noisy places okay, so much of the time. Unless I want to hide away, they are now a part of my ensemble. My shadow Crone has given me another opportunity to let go of judgment and accept everything about who I am.

By contrast, I remember my mother who, when she began to lose her hearing, refused to admit she couldn't hear or to even get her hearing checked. Instead, she stepped more fully into the shadow and was soon being left out of conversations, so she retreated more into her own world. I could never understand why she refused to get hearing aids or even admit this was a problem, but now I am beginning to get it. She made a choice to disappear.

Not only do I not want to disappear, I want to be seen even more now. Again, it's all about making conscious choices. The point is, there are issues to be faced and your strong Crone with her powerful staff will tell you what you need to do next. She will appear in various forms along your path and you only have to be awake enough to recognize her and heed the messages she is offering to you.

One of these opportunities just appeared and I almost missed it. I have had a strong calling to do Crone paintings for quite awhile. Finally, over Winter Solstice break, I got out my paints and did my first painting. It was phenomenal and the painting that appeared is captivating. Recently, I posted her on Facebook and got a lot of positive comments. One in particular, from a new woman friend who is another Crone, stuck with me. She assumed I was a full time artist and asked me if I had submitted my art to We'Moon. I was all ready to explain that I had no time to paint anymore until this book was done, when I stopped and realized my Crone was speaking to me through this new friend. Okay, maybe painting has to happen now, not after the book is done. Who am I to question her wisdom?

Personally, I am more attracted to women who are willing to show both sides. I trust them and want to be around them, because I feel I won't be judged. Those women are my mentors, regardless of their age. How can you be a true mentor and Wise Woman if you don't accept all sides of yourself?

Being a Mentor/Teacher

After attending countless women's groups and gatherings, holding my talking stick in tears while telling my story, facing my pain, self-worth issues and all that baggage of life, over the years, I finally arrived at my last women's gathering in New Zealand. I was 56 and was feeling a shift inside of myself. Instead of experiencing the plethora of emotions bubbling up, I felt a sense of inner quietness and had nothing to say, nothing calling me to the fire so I could cry, scream or tell my story. I watched the 30- and 40-year-olds expressing from those places where I once had been. The energy flowed through their veins; their blood was hot.

One woman in particular, I'll call her Rachel, was very out-spoken and had strong feelings and opinions that she was putting forth, some of which were controversial. As you can imagine, in the rawness of the moment, a few other women were triggered and spoke out from that reactionary place. Rachel just collapsed with what she took as criticism of her very being and rejection of her very soul. In tears, she said she wished she hadn't even come to this event and she was thinking of just packing up and leaving. I could feel the energy pulling her to just get up and run away.

From my quiet place I took all this in, the whole dynamic, and for the first time I felt a calling to speak out. I witnessed myself standing up and speaking directly to Rachel. It was as though the words were coming through me. I saw Rachel for who she was, a strong, empowered woman in her early 30s with all the makings of a real leader. I shared with her: "I see your path as being a trailblazer and one who speaks out. This is often what strong leaders do. This means people will be triggered and project their own issues onto you. This is what happens with all the real leaders. It is so important that you be a mirror and learn how to control your own reactions, so you can allow them to get in touch with their own inner path of personal growth. **If you collapse every time you feel someone is attacking you, then you are being useless and your own power will diminish.** You need to learn this in order to do your work in the world. These woman who are reacting are all gifts for you."

Rachel looked at me, took it in and smiled. She got it!

Afterward I realized that this was my first experience of being an elder. Up until then, I was questioning whether I was done with these circles. Now I could see that not only was I not done, but also my real work was just beginning. It was about me allowing this portal to open, connect with spirit and be a conduit for wisdom if and when it was needed. I was developing that ability to see clearly.

It is a tricky role to be in because there needs to be an absence of ego. If my ego had been running the show, I would have been pushy and it would have been all about me and my expertise. Ugh! I have seen that so many times. And there were times in my past where, in my own insecurity, I had wanted to be seen as someone enlightened. It's a bit embarrassing to admit that, but like Rachel, I had to learn to be centered.

So part of being a Crone mentor is an absence of ego. It is accepting a role and when it's not needed, to gently step back. It's about not being "me" focused. Instead, the focus is on the person you are helping. This is a skill I learned while being a counselor, but this phase of life is taking it to a much deeper level.

Holding the Energy

Certainly, part of being a good teacher/facilitator or any kind of practitioner involves a dynamic called 'holding the energy.' This means being in a witness role, keeping track of all the energies in the room, listening, being aware of what's needed, who is in trouble and which issues aren't being spoken but are being felt. There is also a spiritual element of tuning in to unseen support or invisible but powerful influences that can help you to be in a place of BEINGness, the higher frequencies that can partner with you in your role.

The idea of holding the energy is different for each person but I first learned about this while being a therapist in my earlier career. I learned to trust each person's own process and where they needed to go. I listened and learned to trust my instincts and intuition as to what to say and when to say it. I learned to keep my own ego out of the mix and to be there for my client.

These things were hard for me to learn, especially straight out of graduate school when I was 35. I felt inexperienced and my own issues of needing to be a good counselor were in the forefront. I wanted to be seen as competent. Over time, I realized that all the skills I learned in grad school were way less important than just 'being' with my client.

I attended a ten-day workshop with Ram Dass during that time called Healing the Heart of Compassion. I can see now that it was all about giving us permission to do what he called "being in the cauldron with our client." The important thing was to be a real person first and a practitioner second. In that cauldron there was less of a therapist and client distinction. My only role was to hold the energy and allow the other person to be who they needed to be. It was deep transformational work.

We all hiked into the gorge at Breitenbush Hotsprings, surrounded by old growth forest, chanting in single file. During that three-hour hike, I could feel the nature spirits as they held the energy in this beautiful spot, one of the most magical places on Earth.

Just as in any group, there were people who might unconsciously veer off the trail, disturb the flora or break the silence, and yet, the spirits of that sacred spot would gently bring people back to a place of center and awareness that it is not all about them individually, but about what's best for the whole group, the land, the forest and the spirit world. This special place only exists because the stewards of this land have kept it pristine and allowed it to flourish and exist in the purest form possible.

How can you be a steward of the person you are mentoring or a group you are facilitating? It requires:

- ◎ Being aware of the culture
- ◎ Holding intention and/or creating group intention
- ◎ Being in touch with spirit
- ◎ Setting the stage
- ◎ Creating safety
- ◎ Being a strong presence
- ◎ Listening
- ◎ Witnessing
- ◎ Loving
- ◎ Staying on the path
- ◎ Mindfulness

In a way, everything listed above is Crone energy at its highest vibration. In that magical shift that happens in one's middle to late 50s, after the monthly blood has ended, the role of being a mentor and teacher becomes so much more prominent, and like I experienced in my last women's gathering, suddenly you might be called and find yourself in this role of holding the energy and realizing this is your true role now. The more you recognize and acknowledge it, the more it will start appearing in everything you do.

Looking back, I am now wondering if whenever I operated in that mindset in my 30s, I was accessing my inner Crone, the Wise Woman who naturally has that instinct and ability to step into an egoless place and hold the space for others to do their inner work. I love that thought because as a woman I feel we carry the energy of every developmental stage. There are times I still carry Maiden energy, feeling freer and naive, and likewise when I was 30, the older Wise Woman was my partner many times. She holds that ability to lead and mentor from a deep well of knowing where she taps into the collective unconscious of the wisdom of our ancestors and thousands, if not millions, of women who have stood in these same shoes.

Crones Are Leaders

The Inner Crone's time has now come and we must honor all of her energies: clear sight, strong leadership, full voice, power, strength, inner knowing and insight. In order to access your Inner Crone, you don't have to be age 60 plus. You can be any age and she is also available to men. She brings true Crone Medicine that will help you to speak your truth, get on stage without fear, write that book, lead your team and more.

I wish when I was 25 or 30, someone had told me that I could call up that kind of support from a wise woman elder and she would help me to feel more confident and less insecure, while drawing out my wisdom from an egoless place.

I know now at age 68, I love that I can dance as a Maiden and call on my Earth Mother to help me with being able to work hard and give birth. I need all of those parts to bring this book to light.

New Archetype

We need an entirely new archetype for older women in their Wise Woman years who are expressing their living wisdom and soul through giving birth to their vision, running a business or still doing their life work.

Now, in our Crone years, being juicy means having vitality for what you do. Because patriarchy has been extraordinarily negative to older women, one of my not so secret missions is to take the word Crone and redefine it as an achievement and honored expression. Never has their been a generation like our post-menopausal one. We lived through the birth of the women's liberation movement and have been educating other women ever since. As a juicy Crone, the potential exists for us to change the world we live in, to influence, to redefine, to reinvent, to re-appraise and to make a difference.

My wish for you, visionary women of all ages, is that you are able to embrace and own your unique wisdom and inner beauty so you, too, can be a mentor and know that you are standing in a circle of women. You can look back to who you were and look forward to where you are going. We are here holding our staffs to welcome you.

Ask Your Inner Crone, Elder, Wise Woman

Look in your neighborhood parks and find an old grandmother tree. She will be one of those that has been around for many years, has a solid large trunk and many knots and large branches. She exudes life experience and wisdom. Her roots dive deep into Mother Earth.

Greet and acknowledge her in a way that feels right for you and then sit with her. Ask a question about something where you want great wisdom to help you have more clarity. Ask her for her insight and then listen.

- Listening and waiting is a Crone gift.
- Crones are patient and know there is no hurry.
- Your response might begin with a symbol or a color.
- It might be a whole sentence.
- Take it in, accept it, and say thank you to grandmother tree.
- Leave a blessing for her before you leave.
- It will come from your heart. Trust it.
- Write or draw your insight gift and then put it on your altar at home or in your office.

Wiser and Wilder

My Wild Woman is my muse and when she's flowing, words, colors, ideas, and sounds float out of the river and ride wildly over the rocks to play and frolic in the rapids. Wherever she lands, new greenery sprouts forth and the nature spirits emerge, shiny with inspiration.

At times, the riverbed lays dry and parched, with dying plants gasping for air. My Wild Woman, somewhere in the underworld, feels almost unreachable. My Wisdom, who I count on to connect me to the cosmos, is off playing with Persephone, and yet, in my peripheral vision, I see her and I have to lure her back by going to the edge of her world, into the forest or to an ocean beach, where the two worlds meet.

And then I call her, and slowly the dam breaks and the water begins to flow clear and fresh again. Like magic, the sparkle comes back and I have so much to say, share and create that I have to slow down and let it slowly take shape.

Sometimes it's not easy, in that barren place, to leave my cobwebbed cottage and go out in nature, but this is the key every time. Once I get there and smell the trees, listen to the waves, and hear the birds, she heeds my call. In fact, my wisdom is always my savior and always just a whisper away.

> Bone by bone, hair by hair, Wild Woman comes back. Through night dreams, through events half understood and half remembered. ~Clarissa Pinkola Estés

So, be bold and call on your Wild and Wise Woman. She will come.

I stood on the beach, feeling the sun on my face and the Goddess of the Sea speaking to me. My body was rooted into the sand and I wanted nothing else. It was one of those moments of being present 100 percent with my Wise and Wild Woman.

I was aware of a lineage of ancestors, women upon women who had stood on this same spot in a timeless space of BEINGness. I thanked them for the strength and love they were gifting me. I saw a montage of their faces, filled with wrinkles of wisdom; eyes that could see beyond normal vision into the world of inner sight and calm knowing.

My body was a channel, a hollow bamboo for their energies to fill my soul and make me whole. My Wild Woman wanted to splash in every tide pool, write words in the sand, feel my toes in the water of the tide and call out the sounds of Earth and Sky.

It was one of those moments where everything felt aligned with a vibration of love, flow, clarity and connectedness, all the ways I wish I could be everyday. I know in my deepest truth that operating from this vibration is the most important part of manifesting my own life vision and purpose in the world.

It's my belief that if you can experience something like this even once, it becomes imprinted in your memory. Like me, you will yearn for it every hour of every day. It's like a positive drug that provides the needed environment to grow YOU, who you are meant to be.

It might sound simple but it is so easy to get off-track and get lost while listening to your fears or self doubts instead of your wisdom. In this book, I have shown you the path to creating an environment where you can be the conduit for your own wisdom at every moment. Standing in this space, there is nothing you cannot accomplish.

Sharing the soulful path has been my contribution to the tribe of women, who like me, know you are a here as a conduit for the seeds you are meant to plant in the world during this lifetime. You want your footsteps to make a difference. You too, are part of the line of sisters, mothers and grandmothers who have a vision, and your gift will touch other women and the world in ways you can only imagine.

Mindfulness Going Forward

You each have your purpose and your mission, and you are ready to walk your soulful path and manifest your vision. My message and teaching in the preceding chapters has not been about what you need to do. Most of us are already too busy with Doingness, the frantic energy of following steps to an illusion of success. In that chaotic state, it is so easy to get off track, not listen and become overwhelmed and unclear.

When you look at my Wiser and Wilder Mandala you will see a step-by-step program for you to develop that person who can stand in your own footprints. If you've done the activity at the end of each chapter you will have had some 'AHA' awarenesses already and you will also know which areas are asking you to focus more.

My core focus is about BEINGness which means being who you are authentically, in your real circle, in a balanced and actualized way, with your strong voice, willing to face the unhealed parts of yourself that hold you back.

From a place of standing in a mindful place and connecting with your own wisdom and wildness, the clouds part and the light of your own inner knowing shows up, along with the support of your real mentors, people who will walk that path with you and keep you from getting lost in the woods and forgetting your way.

Your first true mentor is your own soul partner, your Wise Woman who lives in the center of your circle. She is all-knowing and is always there waiting in the shadows of your Doingness.

In order to fulfill your vision and attain the success you want, of course there are many 'doing' actions you will want to incorporate, but this book has been about how to be. From that place, you will make more conscious choices in how you move. Your own Wise Woman is your first partner who will help you to stay awake and aware because she lives in that vibration consistently.

Right now, wherever you are, close your eyes and notice her right out-side of your peripheral vision, or she might be smack dab right in front of you, waiting for you to take notice. Either way, see her and look in her eyes.

Who do you see? Can you feel her presence? She's always with you. It's you who are too lost in your buzzing around to take notice.

It reminds me of my little dog patiently waiting by the door until I notice her looking right at me. All she wants is to go for a walk. Your Wise Woman wants to go on a walk with you too. All you have to do is walk away from your frantic-ness, self-doubt and worry, and take her hand. She will walk you into your own power place where the magic happens.

WISDOM FROM CHAPTER 1: A WOMAN'S WAY

Your Wise Woman's roots are firmly planted in the Woman's Way and she calls you to become a more fully evolved version of yourself.

She encourages you to listen to your soul and make all decisions from that wholistic, intuitive and connective place that you own as a visionary woman.

- How do you tune inward each and every day before you take any actions?
- How do you give yourself permission to transform your natural emotional gifts into intuitive awareness?
- How do you use your inherent wholistic nature to bring a strong overview and balance to everything you do?
- How does your inherent ability to connect to others support your abundant life?
- What is one way you are you feeling stuck right now and how could incorporating these three ways of being help you to move through your issue with new empowerment?

Operating from this mindset will help you stay on your soulful path.

If your immediate response is 'I don't understand how to do this' or 'I don't know,' then the first step is to listen to your emotions behind what your mind is saying. Then bring in your intuition and trust what you hear.

From there you can find people to help you: mentors, peers, or team members to explore it with you. This might include mind mapping and widening your vantage point to include that part of you who is smart and does know and understand.

This is one example of how the Woman's Way triad can help you. Can you think of others?

WISDOM FROM CHAPTER 2: BACK TO YOUR ROOTS

With your Wise Woman support, you will be able to open your voice and tune into your unique song that belongs to no one else. This is your own expression and contribution.

You have important and powerful things to share in the world. Are you ready to express this part of yourself and really go for it?

Your power and voice, combined with others, makes the whole world a better place.

Take your Wild Woman out of hiding and haul her off to a beach or a mountaintop and open your voice fully, calling out. She will feel the primal energy and lets loose. This can feel scary to many women and at first and it might feel like your power is not wholly coming through, but if you let go and do it, you will never hide in the same way again.

I moved past the block of using my whole voice by "calling" while in the shower. The water muffled the sound and helped me feel less exposed.

Here is a song we sang in my women's community (artist unknown). Can you relate to its message?

I am a powerful woman
I have very powerful needs
I have wonderful ideas
I have quite incredible dreams
My dreams tend to come true
They tend to include you
I sense the world is changing
I guess I will change too

We are a powerful people
We have very powerful needs
We have wonderful ideas
We have quite incredible dreams
Our dreams tend to come true
They tend to include you
We sense the world is changing
We guess... we will change too.

We are a powerful people
We have very powerful needs
We have wonderful ideas
We have quite incredible dreams
Our dreams speak of freedom
Freedom speaks from inside
Inside speaks for itself
We've got no reason to hide because

We are a powerful people
We have very powerful needs
We have wonderful ideas
We have quite incredible dreams
Our dreams they will come true
Our dreams they include you
We know the world is changing
We know that we're changing too.

What are your wonderful ideas and dreams? Can you feel your freedom inside? Are you able to connect with that sense of hope within your belly?

WISDOM FROM CHAPTER 3: CIRCLE POWER

It can feel tricky to shift into a BEINGness attitude, especially if you are someone who knows that the entrepreneur side of your house is still un-built. It can bring up so many issues that can throw you off center and into a box, especially when you think about how to learn those busi-nessy parts you lack.

Your next mentors need to be people who get who you are and where you are going. They live in your circle and you trust them.

Ideally they are also listening to their own Wise Woman and so they will encourage you to do the same.

Surrounding yourself with circle energy will help you to stay embedded in the values that support you.

I started a local circle a few years ago called Wise Woman Entrepreneurs here in my community. We meet once a month and it's open to anyone who feels called. We sit in circle where what we do together is less important than how we are together. Can you see and feel how this is so important?

Visionary women want and yearn for circles that are created with this rooted, Wise Woman energy. People leave our circle each time feeling inspired and a sense of relief that this kind of group exists.

One woman shared, "I feel so blessed to have found this group. So many groups are all focused on selling yourself. It's so refreshing to just be and be seen for my real self, with no pretentions."

We share successes and talk about how we overcame challenges. As people learn from each other, it's my belief that every resource we need is accessible in our group.

Is there a circle like this in your community? Can you see how you could begin your own circle that will attract the people who need to be there with you?

The important thing is to get out of any box you are in and find a circle to move to.

I invite you to join our Wiser and Wilder Circle right now. www.facebook.com/wiserandwilder.

WISDOM FROM CHAPTER 4: YOUR SUCCESS PORTAL

You have your Wise and Wild Woman on board, you are coming out of hiding and ready to be seen and heard and you have your circles of power and support. Now it's time to strengthen your business tree by becoming a real visionary entrepreneur.

With both circles overlapped, you will be ready to walk through the almond-shaped doorway that will allow you to give birth to your vision and business as one.

When your visionary and entrepreneurial circles come together, there is an energy that is more powerful than each of them separately and that magic word synergy happens.

Yes, it is this magical, and I know it works, as I shared in this chapter.

Are you willing to step into the process of growing your business as part of your journey of personal growth? The doorway to transformation will allow you to cut loose the cords that are still binding you to your less powerful version of yourself.

- ⊚ Can you see how your creativity and vision will be less realized without you doing your inner work?
- ⊚ What kind of circles and mentors do you need in order to walk through that portal?
- ⊚ Can you imagine yourself on the other side?
- ⊚ Are you willing to see yourself as an equally balanced visionary and entrepreneur?

WISDOM FROM CHAPTER 5: SOULFUL COMMUNITY

Your next step is to nurture the three layers of your community: your soul partner, your golden team and your supportive people.

In a garden, plants thrive when they are in groups. One lonely plant has less chances of doing well. Your business has to be larger than just you.

- ◉ Are you ready to see your dreams bigger?
- ◉ Who cares about you and wants more connection with you?
- ◉ Who can you say yes to and how can you build that relationship stronger?

What is one thing you can do right now to expand your soulful community so it becomes an intentional strong force in your life?

What kind of support do you need to shift into being a person who can build soulful community?

WISDOM FROM CHAPTER 6: BREAKING FREE

This chapter is about liberating what has been holding you back from your magnificence.

In this section, I talked about calling your soul back and rescuing your Wild Woman from wherever she has been left. In order to move forward, you need her as an ally.

You may have been trying to fit in and felt cut-off from your own wisdom.

This is where you can embrace your Wounded Healer, the one who is so skilled at helping others.

When you find your Wild Woman, you will see that she offers both soul wisdom and practical wisdom. You need both.

- ◉ What has been your ritual for finding this part of yourself?
- ◉ Are you ready to bring her back 100% and throw away the cage?

WISDOM FROM CHAPTER 7: BEING MONEY WISE

Once you have done all the other work of breaking free and standing in your circle, along comes the real test of your leadership and empowerment.

You might be like many brilliant women who know that in order to touch more people and make a bigger difference, you need to let go of financial struggle and learn how to be a strong money manager.

Can you see how this is the next piece on your journey around the circle?

You can only do so much toward making the big difference without facing your money Wise Woman who grows into prosperity by learning how to be responsible.

In this chapter, I shared how important it is to know your money story and realize that you can face your money wounds and change into an abundant woman who can help thousands of people instead of only a handful.

- ◉ Can you see how becoming money wise will help you personally as well as professionally?
- ◉ How do your money issues hold you back?
- ◉ What is your plan that will change your money story?

WISDOM FROM CHAPTER 8: SEASONS AND CYCLES

In this point of the journey, it's important to come back to the grounded place of remembering that you are a woman first and foremost, before you became a visionary and before you ever decided to become an entrepreneur.

Your fertility path and the moon defines your developmental stages of Maiden, Mother and Crone. Understanding these stages provides a way for you to accept who you are and how that characterizes the way you stand, plus other personal issues as they overlap onto your business choices.

I hope you enjoyed seeing yourself on the river and it gave you some insight about the way you see the world and your own life in the lineage of women. Seeing your business through this lens, as well as all the others I've presented, can be enlightening and offer you new perspectives.

- ◎ How were you able to see yourself in a more distinct way?
- ◎ Based on where you are in your own seasons and cycles, how does this affect your perspective right now?
- ◎ What is your business telling you about its own fertility cycle? Is it a freshly sown seed or an old cherry tree with many gnarled branches?

WISDOM FROM CHAPTER 9: CRONE MEDICINE

The Crone is the teacher and mentor, so it's perfect that she holds the roots of this book.

In her pure egoless form, she has held the deep vision for this whole venture. The Wise and Wild Woman lives in her being and from that place, the Crone knows who she is and can see clearly what I often can't or don't see. I thank her everyday for standing by my side and encouraging me to own these parts of myself.

A Crone is more than an elder. She is one who knows and walks the path of spirit. She accepts and is accepting without judgment. It doesn't mean she has no opinions; she might have a lot to say and most often is blunt and doesn't mince words. She chooses to be conscious in this way.

She is witness and allows others to do and be who they are. She doesn't always care if she looks or acts a certain way. She just is. So in a way, her presence is a perfect way to end this book as she is pure BEINGness nurtured by self-acceptance.

She is the one who will change the world to a better place. Her visions embody all of your visions and she has the capacity to hold it all and be juicy, crazy, wild, ugly and powerful as the moment demands.

She is the one who partnered me in writing this book so it is dedicated to her and that place in each of you, regardless of your age.

All you have to do is ask her what her gift is for you and then listen.

Wild Visionary Credos for Life

Find your circle

Be visible

Create, write, dance

Surround yourself with big trees

Step onto your stage and shine

Open your voice and rant

Listen to your inner crone

Uncage your Wild Woman

Embody happiness

About Kaya

Kaya Singer is a Wise Woman entrepreneur, mentor, artist, and writer. She helps women discover how to empower themselves and others, and to fully manifest their visionary businesses.

Having never fit into a traditional business box, Kaya's been self-employed for over 40 years, growing in confidence and clarity around her own life vision.

At first she was as an artist and then became a psychotherapist before finally opening her present business, Awakening Business LLC, in her mid 50s.

Supported by the strong circles she's created, her wisdom touches thousands of women through mentoring, women's gatherings and mastermind retreats, in both the United States and in New Zealand, where she lived for 12 years.

Kaya's mission continues to be helping vision-ary women wake up, stop hiding and invest in themselves so they can become who they are meant to be in the world. Now growing into her Crone wisdom years, she's come full circle and is has integrated her art and coaching business into one.

When not working with clients, she paints in the studio she shares with her husband, plays with clay, dances to 60s music or spends time out in the forest or at the ocean. She loves pure nature and this is where her Wild Woman thrives and reconnects to Mother Earth.

Featured Wise and Wild Women

Huge thanks to the wonderful women who so willingly shared their stories and contributed their wisdom to this book. I so honor each of them for their gifts and willingness to share from their heart.

Jennifer Lee – RightBrainBusinessPlan.com

Rebecca Skeele – RebeccaESkeele.com

Michele Grace Lessirard – SharedJourneys.org

Katie Cavanaugh – katiecavanaugh.com

Nancy Swisher – NancySwisher.com

Luna Jaffe – LunaJaffe.com

Flora Bowley – FloraBowley.com

Téa Silvestre Godfrey – StoryBistro.com

Kathleen Hanagan – TurnOnYourLight.com

Aine Dee – wealthreimagined.com

Jocelyn Mozak – MozakDesign.com

Lindsey Dawson – LindseyDawson.com

With Gratitude

My wonderful Golden Team helped make Wiser and Wilder come to life. Lisa Canfield was my beginning book coach and helped me realize that I actually did have a lot to say. My dear friend and editor Sally Philips kept me sane and focused as the chapters unfolded, with her amazing ability to carry overview and detail all at once. Deandra Ellerbe brought in her beautiful eye for book design and in our first meeting I knew she got who I was.

My mastermind buddies, Téa Silvestre Godfrey, Sonia Miller, and Joanne McCall helped me stay on track and their feedback, support, and love have helped me to trust my own instincts and step more fully into listening and trusting my own wisdom.

I want to also give a huge thanks to my sweet clients, friends, and colleagues who have cheered me along the way with their supportive comments, excitement, and sharings, from beginning to end. There are too many people to name, but you know who you are and I couldn't have done this without you. This books belongs to all of us.

Thanks to my coach, Andrea J. Lee who sat at my kitchen table with me and said, "You need to write a book," and all my cronies in the Lab who witnessed my transformation and held the space for me to Be.

My husband Wayne Singer deserves a special thank you for allowing me to be Crazy Woman and still love me through it all. Lastly my son Robin, who a visionary "male" entrepreneur and has always believed in me and helped me to see how this book will also touch many visionary men.

Stay Connected to Our Circle

If you loved this book you'll want to know how to stay connected with us! We are all about community and there are many ways for you to join us.

◎ Join our Facebook group – facebook.com/groups/WiserandWilder/

◎ Join one of our amazing Wiser and Wilder weekend retreats for Visionary women.

   For information and dates – WiseWomenRetreats.com

◎ Contact me about coming to your city to offer a workshop – kaya@kayasinger.com

◎ Get private mentoring to help you develop your vision into a successful business – awakeningbusiness.com/

◎ Listen to my ongoing podcast: "Business the Wise Woman Way" on iTunes and Stitcher Radio.

Thanks for being on this path with us.
It's magical!

Made in the USA
San Bernardino, CA
31 May 2020